COOL careers

for girls

in

Cybersecurity and National Safety

COOL careers

for girls

in

Cybersecurity and National Safety

LINDA THORNBURG

Library of Congress Cataloging-in-Publication Data

Thornburg, Linda, 1949-
  Cool careers for girls in cybersecurity and national safety / Linda Thornburg.
    p. cm.--(Cool careers for girls; 14)
  Includes bibliographical references and index.
  ISBN 1-57023-208-3 paper
  ISBN 1-57023-209-1 hardcover

                                                                    2003113211

Publisher: For information on Impact Publications, including current and forthcoming publications, authors, press kits, bookstore, and submission requirements, visit Impact's Web site: www.impactpublications.com

Publicity/Rights: For information on publicity, author interviews, and subsidiary rights, contact the Public Relations and Marketing Department: Tel. 703/361-7300 or Fax 703/335-9486.

Sales/Distribution: All paperback bookstore sales are handled through Impact's trade distributor: National Book Network, 15200 NBN Way, Blue Ridge Summit, PA 17214, Tel. 1-800-462-6420. All other sales and distribution inquiries should be directed to the publisher: Sales Department, IMPACT PUBLICATIONS, 9104-N Manassas Dr., Manassas Park, VA 20111-5211, Tel. 703/361-7300, Fax 703/335-9486, or E-mail: info@impactpublications.com

Book design by Guenet Abraham
Desktopped by Brad Boyd

Contents

Cybersecurity and National Safety Careers

A Special Introduction by Lisa Daniel

Do you like the idea of protecting the nation's safety? How about people's money? Or the buildings they work and do business in? How about the personal information people sometimes send across the Internet, such as identification numbers? All those things are protected every day by tens of thousands of people who work in security and related fields. In the fast-growing fields of cybersecurity and national safety, you can have a job working to protect almost anything. In this book you will read about women with diverse backgrounds and skills who have one thing in common: They work to protect people and things.

Jobs in security are more plentiful than ever because of increasing threats to people and to important parts of our nation's infrastructure—computer networks, buildings, bridges, and transportation and water systems. Threats and the potential for damage have increased in recent years—strangely enough, partly because of improved technology. Although the Internet and personal computers add convenience to our lives, they also make it easier for people to commit crimes, such as stealing personal information, sometimes known as identity theft, or information from businesses, often called corporate espionage. Technology also makes it easier to tap into secret or classified information, such as the hacking of government computer files, and to pass along illegal pictures like child pornography or information that helps terrorist groups.

The problem of identity theft was highlighted in November 2002. Two employees of a computer company with headquarters in Long Island, New York, were charged with stealing and selling the personal information of more than 30,000 Americans. The accused allegedly used their access to computer passwords to obtain information from credit bureaus, which hold important information about anyone who has a credit card or has ever gotten a loan to buy a house or a car. The victims of the identity theft together lost millions of dollars, and must undergo the difficult process of restoring their good names to those companies that might lend them money.

Terrorism, which threatens a nation's government and its citizens, increased throughout the 1990s. In the United States, it reached a severe crisis point on Sept. 11, 2001, when terrorists hijacked jet airliners and flew them into the World Trade Center in New York City, and into the Pentagon in Arlington, Virginia, killing more than 3,000 people. Shortly after this terrible incident, five people died and several more became sick when letters laced with the deadly bacteria anthrax were mailed through the U.S. Postal Service. The terrorism of that autumn caused us to look at certain security procedures more closely. Airports and airlines began checking passengers and baggage more closely. Public arenas like sports stadiums and concert halls were assigned many more uniformed officers.

The Many Faces of Security

The women in this book were practicing security in quieter, less visible ways for years before terrorism struck the United States. They include a mechanical engineer who helped to develop a machine that detects the bacteria anthrax; a computer engineer in the U.S. Navy who oversees the security of the military's computers; an intelligence analyst for the U.S. Customs Service who monitors the Internet for crimes; businesswomen who consult and train others on how to protect the information stored on computers and computer networks; a security manager at a company that makes digital video recorders; a computer security specialist at the U.S. Treasury Department; a sociologist who testifies in court about whether a business had enough security when a crime was committed; a biomedical engineer whose research will make it easier to communicate during catastrophes; and a woman who helps create security policies for a major airline. The diversity of these women is a reflection of the security industry itself. Many parts of our society are interconnected and it takes many different types of experts to prevent disaster.

"That is the wonderful thing," says Marene Allison, director of security for Avaya, a New Jersey-based communication network management company. "You can be anything from a military person to an accountant to a chemist or biologist or even a history major. You can try your first love and if it doesn't work out, security has so many areas you can move into. And when you go from being a security guard to being a chief security officer of a major corporation, you have such a diverse skill set that you can do almost anything in the field."

Allison, a West Point graduate and former FBI agent, raises an important point about the need for various types of people in security. Although security began as a law enforcement field where police academies and criminal justice degrees were the accepted forms of education, the field is no longer so limited. While there's still a need for people with law enforcement backgrounds, particularly in the area of physical security, which tends to be less technical and protects structures such as buildings, bridges, and transportation systems, there is an even greater need for people with computer skills. People who are computer savvy can work not only in the field of logical security, the protection of computers and computer information, but any place that computers are used—which is almost everywhere! A third area of the industry is national security. An example of how all three of these areas interconnect was seen after Sept. 11, 2001. Terrorism is a national security problem, but it can be carried out in many different ways: against buildings, public transportation, public water systems, or computers that operate those facilities and almost every other part of our nation's infrastructure. Many computer systems link offices together, causing a domino effect from a single mishap. For example, if computers are disabled in an emergency dispatch center, it could shut down the ability of police, firefighters, and rescue workers to respond quickly to a major disaster. The lack of communications also could slow the readiness of emergency rooms to respond and the media to quickly alert the public.

"Security is blending. It's not the old cops security stuff anymore," says Allison. "Today all the fields are quickly merging. There's nowhere today that doesn't include technology. You have access controls and computer systems everywhere. They all provide you clues to potential threats."

National Funding For Computer Security Education

Potential threats to computers and the information they hold, as well as concerns about having enough professionals in the security field, led Congress in November 2002 to pass The Cyber Security Research and Development Act. The law will expand federal funding by giving $903 million per year, for five years, to the National Science Foundation for the creation of cybersecurity research centers. It also will provide money for college under-

graduate (associate's and bachelor's degree) programs and support partnerships between colleges and businesses, sponsored by the National Institute of Standards and Technology. In passing the legislation, Congress realized that today more than 72 million American workers, about two out of every five, use computers at work, many of them for e-mail and the Internet.

Pat Gilmore is a senior security consultant for some of the world's 50 largest companies. She works at Red Siren Technology in California. She is the treasurer of (ISC)2, an international certification organization that credentialed her as a Certified Information Systems Security Professional (CISSP). Certifications are important in the industry and are offered by several professional organizations. To become certified in a given area, a professional must meet certain academic or professional requirements, pay several hundred dollars to the organization, then pass a test in the given subject area.

Gilmore, a French major who began her career in banking, says the large number of American workers who use computers makes security a good industry for those who like to work with others. "Security is all about people," she says. "The best security people understand that you have to change people's behavior to secure data. People, processes, and technology are the main components of security, with people being the most important. All employees of a company have to work together to protect security. That's because every employee who comes into contact with company information has a responsibility to protect what he or she knows."

Unfortunately, Gilmore says, studies have shown that some young people don't enter the information security field (which she notes is about all information and not just that stored on computers) because they believe they won't have much contact with other people. "Some of it may be isolating if you're in a highly technical area," she says. "But if you're in risk management where you're talking with others about security risks, that is not isolating. You work closely with people and use your creative juices to come up with clever ways to help companies. That's how I've spent my career!"

Bob Johnston, CISSP, the manager of credentialing for (ISC)2 at its headquarters in Framingham, Massachusetts, began his career 30 years ago in a highly technical and isolated area of computers. Information technology gave him a wonderful background to move into information security where he has more contact with people. "Information technology, generally, keeps you buried," he says. "You're caught in a hall of geeks. Information security has me working with every department and working with people all day. I love it. It's so diverse; it's always changing. No two days are the same."

Some of the most important jobs in security may seem dry on the surface, Johnston says, but they are rewarding once you know what has to be done and how to do it. One of the fastest growing areas of information security is known as "governance," which refers to the overall management of all information in a given area, such as company procedures. While "there is a humdrum side" to governance, Johnston says, it is "an extremely important area" that places the security professional in the circle of senior managers.

For governance and most other areas of information security, an undergraduate business degree and even a master's in Business Administration with an emphasis on technology are a good way to start your career, Johnston says. "Some of the best computer security people I've seen are those who understand the process of management. You can't secure what you don't understand."

Security is a balancing act in which security professionals must weigh the pros and cons. For example, if a company that only does business on the Internet requires users to go through so many security screenings that they find it a hassle to shop there, people will stop using the site. "We can always secure an industry, but we can also put them out of business," Johnston says. "You need that business understanding so that security is adequate, rather than perfect. This is about risks versus benefit."

That doesn't mean that security professionals with their eye on management can skip the technical functions, says Allison, who is an executive for a private company. "I'm not going to build a (computer) firewall (which protects the computer network from intrusions). But I better know how it's built and who is building it."

Shirley Pierini, CPP, is a Certified Protection Professional through the American Society of Industrial Security, and a security consultant with Sako & Associates, Security System Design, near Los Angeles. Pierini is a former police officer with a bachelor's degree in Business Administration and a master's in Security Management. Her background in law enforcement and business has allowed her to move back and forth from policing to corporate management, where she has secured both important people and buildings. "It's typical to move in this industry, if you want to get ahead," she says. "You have to be flexible and willing to accept opportunities as they come along."

Additionally, Pierini says, you have to stand up for yourself and demand a top salary. She began earning more than $100,000 a year about ten years ago. "Any person in security management should be making six figures," she says.

Even more important than a big salary, Pierini says, the work stays exciting. "What I like most is the adrenaline rush. It's never boring. I have to think on my feet continuously. As benign as a building may seem, it's always a challenge to secure it."

Getting Started Now

This book is a good place to begin your research on cybersecurity and national safety careers. The stories of the women told here will give you a good idea of the educational requirements and the challenges and rewards of many different types of security and related careers. You also will learn that some of these women made their career choices when they were girls, while some waited a long time to decide on a career. Along with each story, you'll find a checklist with some clues about what type of personality would be suitable for a particular job. Information about salaries and employment opportunities also is provided. Check resources at your library for up-to-date salary information.

The last chapter, Getting Started On Your Own Career Path, gives you advice from the women profiled about what you can do now to explore a career in security, identifies helpful reading materials and websites, and lists organizations you can contact for additional information.

Lisa Daniel is a Washington-area freelance journalist who has written frequently about security issues.

Mandy Andress

Mandy Andress

Security Manager, TiVo

Major in Business Administration; master's degree in Management Information Systems, Business Administration College, Texas A&M University, College Station, Texas

Security
Manager

The Architect of Computer Security

Mandy Andress works for one of her favorite companies—TiVo. TiVo provides software you can buy to record television programs on a hard disk and then watch them on your TV. As TiVo's security manager Mandy is responsible for protecting all TiVo's data and computer systems from hackers, computer worms, computer viruses, and other security dangers.

One of Mandy's responsibilities is to install and update firewalls, software that protects TiVo's computer network from hackers who might enter through the network connection to the Internet. "I have to plan so that engineers (who need their computers to work) aren't stuck without use of the computer network while I'm working on it. That takes a lot of coordination."

Information Technology Audit Professional

Can earn $40,000 to $50,000 right out of college. Security administrators make between $60,000 and $100,000. For security consultants, depends on experience and how hard you are willing to work. Security managers and chief security officers can make $100,000 and up.

Mandy also is responsible for formulating the company's computer security policy. "We have to be clear about what our security posture is, what we will and won't allow, and how we will enforce our policy. For example, engineers can't put hacking tools

Another of Mandy's jobs is to put security "patches" (bits of computer code that protect against the vulnerabilities that a software manufacturer discovers after the company has released software to the public) on the company's computer servers (that

I'm not happy when I'm sitting still and not learning anything, whether it's useless trivia or random bits of information or something immediately useful.

(to break into computer systems) on the system and they can't run streaming media (pictures and sound sent over the computer network) unless the manager says there is a business purpose."

network the computers together) and on desktop and laptop computers. The patches help protect the engineers' computers from the latest computer security dangers.

Works at Deloitte and
▼ Touche, accounting
   systems security

Moves to Ernst and
▼ Young, information
   security

Works in security
▼ administration,
   Privada and Evant

TiVo has about 300 employees so Mandy has a busy job trying to make sure all the computers are secure. But if she didn't do this work, a hacker could intrude into the network and spy on, destroy, or change information. A computer virus could cause the network to go down. If that happened, the engineers would lose a lot of productive work time.

"Many times security people are seen as a hindrance. When we have to add security to the system it disrupts employees' daily tasks and makes them have to work longer. So the challenge with computer security is trying to make the end users aware that they are part of the process and it's not a hindrance to them but, rather, it helps to protect them. It will prevent them from losing a lot more work time if the system were to get blown up by a computer virus or somebody would break into it and change or delete their work."

Needs to be Persuasive

Mandy has to convince TiVo executives it is worth spending the money to put in secure computer architecture. "A lot of management find security to be just a cost center; they don't see the real value of it. It's pretty much like buying insurance because you are trying to protect yourself from the 'what if'. All these 'what ifs' have a percentage of likelihood that they will occur. If a 'what if' has a likelihood of happening only one percent of the time and it would cost a million dollars to protect against it, we'll take

MANDY'S CAREER PATH

Starts ArcSec
Technologies,
writes book

Security manager
at TiVo

the risk and hope it doesn't happen. But if there is a 99 percent chance that the next computer virus that comes out will hit us, we obviously want to spend the money to help protect ourselves from that risk. I have to understand how to talk to top management and present the information in a way they will understand. My job is to present the risks and the costs to protect against these risks. Then it's up the executives to make the decision that the risk is worth protecting against.

"I also have to understand how to talk to users to make them see that they are part of the process, that it's not that we are against them or trying to make them less effective in their work, but that we want to work with them to make their computers more secure."

The most challenging aspect of Mandy's work is that the security issues are always changing. New dangers appear every day. It's a cat-and-mouse game, where hackers come up with a new form of attack and the security experts figure out how to protect against it. Then the hackers come up with another method of attack. There is always something new to learn.

Consultant and Author

Besides working at TiVo, Mandy also runs her own company called ArcSec Technologies. She started ArcSec about three years ago to do computer security consulting and analysis of security products and services. Currently Mandy is working on two new projects for ArcSec. One involves testing firmware (the operating system for smaller computing devices like personal digital assistants, faxes, and printers) for security-related issues. Mandy's client is a well-known company. "They send me updates or releases of one of their main products as they develop these, and I test them for possible security vulnerabilities. One big focus today in firmware is making the security configuration easier for the end user. So I'm testing that and sending my feedback and comments on ways I think they could improve how they are presenting the information about security to the end user."

Mandy also currently is analyzing how competitive the product of a company that makes vulnerability assessment software is compared with other companies which make similar products. This software goes out and checks the computer network to identify what operating system is running and what security vulnerabilities exist. Then it writes a report on the vulnerabilities and suggests ways to fix them.

CAREER CHECKLIST ✓

You'll like this job if you ...

- Have a real love of knowledge and learning

- Are fascinated by technology and what people can make with it

- Are independent and won't let anybody tell you what you can and can't do

- Will explore and learn technology on your own

- Can be persuasive and convincing

- Like to write

"I have a lab set up in my house that has about 40 different devices. I run these products against all these devices to see how they perform—how fast they are, how detailed the reports are, what vulnerabilities they identify, how accurate they are at identifying what operating systems are running, to see how different products compare to the product of my client."

Mandy does most of her work for ArcSec on evenings and weekends. Besides working with companies that make security-related products or products that need to have security built into them, she also consults with companies about what products would work best for them to make their computer systems secure. She purchased her laboratory equipment using money she made from her consulting.

Mandy is the author of a book called *Surviving Security: How to Integrate People, Process, and Technology*, which is for anyone who has to understand information technology security. The book is being used as a textbook in college computer security classes. She's now working on an updated edition of the book. She also writes articles about security products for computer-related publications.

"One of the best ways to establish yourself as an expert is to write product reviews. It keeps you up to date and it gets you the products so you can play with them and see what they really can do instead of having to rely on the company's website." Mandy publishes some of her reviews on her own website, http://www.survivingsecurity.com.

Loves Computers From an Early Age

Born in Houston, the daughter of a chemical salesman, Mandy and her family moved to eastern Pennsylvania when she was five. It was in Pennsylvania that she first got exposed to computers, when her dad brought one home for her. "I loved it and quickly picked up how to write programs and make it do other strange things." Then in elementary school Mandy was in a pilot program of computer classes. "When they offered more classes I took them. They were always fun. My brother and I had computers as a hobby growing up, playing with them, taking them apart, seeing what they did, and understanding how they worked."

I taught myself how the computer works. There weren't any classes in that when I was in school. By the time I got to my master's degree in college, I had already taught myself most of what I needed to know.

In high school Mandy decided she would like to be an accountant. She later went to Texas A&M University and studied accounting. "The Internet was taking off and I was always playing with computers. In the last year of my undergraduate degree at Texas A&M I started to see the combination of computers and accounting. I took a class in systems of accounting and it was fun. My professor saw that I liked it a lot and said, 'You should really look into accounting systems and computers'. Then I had an internship at Exxon (an oil and gas company) and they placed me in the audit department. That's where I saw the first real merger of accounting and information systems, how they all fit to-gether. That shifted my focus from being a straight accountant/auditor to having the business background but applying it to computer systems."

Financial accounting systems that are computer-based need to be protected against security breaches. "The auditors rely on the numbers in the reports generated by these systems. They need to make sure there are proper controls so people can't just go in and add or change or delete data. I made sure that we had the proper change control and that the data was encrypted. It was very high level security, but it gave me a good general overview of how everything worked."

Works in Accounting

After getting her master's degree from Texas A&M in computer science, Mandy went to work at Deloitte and Touche, a big accounting firm. "After a while, just doing security control became monotonous. I continued to play with computers at home, getting more and more technical and understanding how firewalls worked and how to configure virtual private networks (spaces on the Internet that can't be accessed by anyone who doesn't have the right password and other credentials). I wanted to get more hands-on experience in the technical area and Deloitte and Touche didn't have the ability to offer me that so I went to work for Ernst and Young (another big accounting firm) in Palo Alto, California."

At Ernst and Young, Mandy was hired to help clients with their information security needs. "It was a small, bright team of people and I just kind of jumped in and absorbed as

GROUNDBREAKERS
Computer Entrepreneur

Sandra Kurtzig (1960-) When she was a 25-year-old housewife and mother of two, Sandra Kurtzig began writing software to earn extra income. Ten years later she had built ASK, a 200-employee company that has earned more than $22 million in sales for its business information systems.

Source: Patently Female

much of that information as I possibly could. So I learned a lot of the basics of what I know now. That's where I got started in the testing laboratory. They had a lab that I began managing and began getting products into. We would have companies that wanted certain things, and we would build them in the lab and then bring them to the company and show them how they worked and help them decide what they really needed."

At the height of the Internet boom, when Northern California was an area where many companies using Internet technology were started, Mandy left Ernst and Young to become the director of security for a company called Privada. Privada, one of the companies started during this "dotcom" era, quickly went out of business. Mandy moved from Privada, where she had found it hard to do what she needed to do to protect the company's computer network because the executives didn't really believe in the need for comprehensive computer security, to Evant Solu-

tions. This company had a service for the retail industry that it offered over the Internet. Mandy worked to build up the company's security architecture, but when the company changed its business model to provide a product rather than a service through the Internet, it laid off 75 percent of its workforce and Mandy was among those who lost their jobs.

Then Mandy began working full time on ArcSec projects. She had started her company when she was working at Privada. Later she saw the job at TiVo listed on an e-mail newsletter on security issues. She decided to apply because she had a TiVo and thought it would be fun to work for the company.

Mandy says she is "leading, not bleeding edge. I watch the trends. It's usually about six months from the time that I pick up on a trend to where it becomes common knowledge in the industry." Right now a trend that Mandy is seeing is something called event correlation. "Companies have different devices for security—firewalls, intrusion detection system, computer servers that have security alerts and generate notice, but there is no real way to correlate all this information and understand what's really going on. A whole host of products which do that correlation has popped up recently. All your devices and systems send their logs and alerts and messages to one central system. It culls through all these and analyzes them to understand what's going on. It helps you get a better picture of what's really happening on your network."

When Mandy isn't working, she likes to analyze movies—how they are made and what the cinematography is like—and she likes to mountain bike and hike in the beautiful San Francisco Bay area.

Sue McGrath

Sue McGrath

Chief Research Engineer, Institute for Security Technology Studies, Dartmouth College, Hanover, NH

Major in Electrical Engineering; master's degree in Biomedical Engineering, Rutgers University, New Brunswick, NJ; Ph.D. in Biomedical Engineering, Rutgers

Combat Casualty Care
and Emergency Response Researcher

Her Research Will Help Save Lives

Dr. Sue McGrath's job as a researcher involves using "mobile code," a new type of computer technology. Sue is working on a computer and biomedical research project that will help army medics and those who are first to respond to emergencies, such as paramedics, firemen, and police. Sue is the lead researcher in emergency management and response research for the Institute for Security Technology Studies at Dartmouth College.

She and her group of researchers are working to build computer systems that will give army medics, "first responders," and other emergency management workers information about an emergency—when it oc-

Biomedical Researcher

A researcher with a B.S. degree would likely make in the neighborhood of $50,000 to $60,000. With an M.S. degree, you can make between $60,000 and $80,000 and with a Ph.D., $80,000 to $120,000.

SUE'S CAREER PATH

▼ Discovers her
first control system,
the heart, in fourth grade

▼ Studies electrical
engineering at Drexel

▼ Works as civilian
electrical engineer
for the Navy

curred, what's going on, and how the consequences are spreading.

Sue's team is working on computerized sensors (tiny computers) that will be put on the injured and on emergency response workers so these people can be located more easily in an emergency, such as the devastation that occurred at the World Trade Center on September 11, 2001. Soldiers in battle can wear the sensors so that medics can monitor their physiological status and perform effective triage. The sensors use a new technology to route the information they collect about the people wearing them to an information management system. A medic, paramedic, nurse, or doctor can look at the vital signs of the injured person—heart rate, the amount of oxygen in the blood, and how well the blood is circulating throughout the body—to see who needs treatment first.

The work Sue's group does will give those who treat victims of catastrophes information to make better decisions. Doctors, paramedics, and other health care workers involved in emergency care will be able to tell how many injured there are and how serious the injuries are so that they can determine where the injured should be treated and what the next step in fighting the disaster should be.

The technology used in this type of computer system is a wireless technology, but in some ways it differs from other wireless computer networks, like those used for cell phones. A small computing device (the sensor on the injured person) transmits the

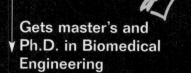
Gets master's and
Ph.D. in Biomedical
Engineering

Marries Dennis, has
son and daughter

Works on mobile
code computing at
Lockheed Martin

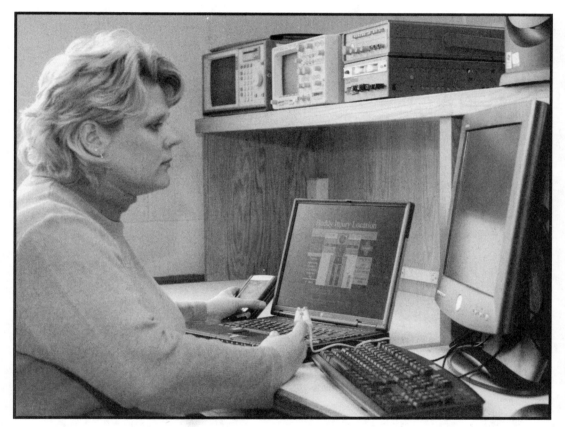

information (a patient's vital signs) using something called "mobile code," which is a certain algorithm, to another computing device, such as a personal digital assistant carried by a first responder. The information from the first responder's PDA then can be routed to a bigger computer after being viewed. The bigger computer will process the information at the

SUE'S CAREER PATH

Hired by Dartmouth's
Thayer School of
Engineering

Researches how sensors
can be used in emergency
management

level of complexity needed. The bits of mobile code that route the information are "smart"—they can remember the information until they can safely transfer it and they wait until a connection opens up to where they are supposed to go. They can adjust themselves to whatever computing environment exists at the time.

"It's a more robust way of communicating in these ad hoc networks, where there are no wires between machines, there is not a lot of bandwidth,

In my career it was not always evident to me at the time that there would be benefits to me for the work that I was doing. I made the decisions that were right for me at the time and it has led me to where I want to be. It's important to understand where you want to go, but to understand it's not always going to be a single-step process.

and people are moving around constantly so the topography of the network is always changing," Sue says.

The technology originally was developed for the U.S. military to use on battlefields where logistical and tactical information is distributed to soldiers and decision makers.

"This is the first time in my career that I have been able to independently direct my own research. Previously I worked for the Navy doing research, but that research had to match the Navy's mission, and the same thing was true when I worked for a private company. We had certain core areas and our research was related to them and to our customers' needs. Now, if I can write a proposal and get funding, I can research whatever interests me, as long as it meets the mission of the Institute.

"The sensor research was something I decided that I wanted to do. I wrote a proposal that emphasized the military applications, and I was able

CAREER CHECKLIST ✓

You'll like this job if you ...

Like math and science

Want to know how things work

Can think logically

Have the self-confidence you will need to defend your ideas

Will not be afraid to speak in front of both large and small groups of people

Can be persuasive and will be able to lead and manage other people to convince people in the medical field that this was something that needed to be done and that we at the Institute were the right people to do it. It was very exciting to start from scratch in a project area that I'm interested in and to be able to create a prototype of the system. There may also be a lot of things that can be done with this system in the areas of monitoring elderly or disabled people at home and monitoring people who have had surgery."

Besides directing and doing research, Sue has many other responsibilities at Dartmouth. Her work falls into three categories: research, administration, and teaching. Sue likes the research part of her job best, although she enjoys the variety that teaching and her other duties provide.

Keeping the Country Safe

The Institute, originally funded by the U.S. government for three years after a terrible bombing of a government building in Oklahoma City, conducts research to keep computer networks and the country's infrastructure (such as its medical systems, transportation systems, and law enforcement systems) secure. Some researchers who report to Sue

Try to do the best where you are at the time, while still keeping an eye on your next goal. I was very impatient when I was younger, but as I got older I learned to take things a little slower and enjoy what I am doing at the moment.

are working on a project that involves an intrusion detection system for computer networks. This system tracks when an unauthorized person accesses a computer network and then correlates the data from these types of incidents, so that researchers can see where attacks (for example, attacks on the Internet) are happening and suggest ways to stop them.

Part of Sue's job is to guide this group of researchers and to help determine their priorities. She also has to find ways to get funding for the research. She writes proposals to get research grants from organizations that might be interested in the type of cybersecurity and infrastructure protection research done at the Institute. She has to disburse the money allocated for research to members of her research group for equipment and supplies. She helps decide what it's most important to spend the money on.

Teaching Responsibilities

Sue teaches three days a week. She works for Dartmouth's Thayer School of Engineering. Right now she is teaching a graduate course in computer architecture. It is about how computers can be put together for special projects, a field Sue enjoys but has not studied extensively. It takes her between eight and 12 hours to prepare for every hour of lecture she delivers to her class. She also has to be available to the students in her class a certain number of hours a week, in case they have questions about the subject or the work they are completing for the course. Next semester Sue will teach an undergraduate course on developing secure computer systems. The course will cover what hackers do, how they work, and how to make a computer system more secure. Usually Sue spends between 40 and 50 hours a week in various activities related to teaching.

"The teaching helps me in my research, because I get to learn more about areas that I'm researching. I'm not obligated to teach, but Dartmouth asked me and I really enjoy working with the students. It's a lot of fun. The first year I came to Dartmouth they asked me to teach, but I didn't want to because my children were three and four at the time and I wanted to make sure I got my family through the transition period of moving and that I spent as much time with them as I could."

These days Sue and her husband, who also works at the Thayer School of Engineering, are up early each day so they can juggle kids and work responsibilities. Sue begins her day about 6:00 a.m. when she gets breakfast for her son and daughter and helps them get ready for school. As soon as the family is out of the house Sue starts her own work, checking her notes for her computer architecture class or answering e-mail. Then she goes to class. After class she usually has meetings on research proposals.

If not, she does administrative work like reviewing budgets and answering e-mail. At 2:00 p.m. she picks up her kids from school and gets them started on some activity, after which she puts in another hour or two doing some writing, preparing for her lectures, or grading papers. She spends time with her family in the evening, and, after the kids go to bed, does another hour or two of work. On the days when she isn't teaching she is researching. "I work on the weekends many times so I can get everything done. It's not always easy, but my husband helps out and we make it work."

Fascinated With the Cardiovascular System

Sue first realized she really liked science in the fourth grade when the class began to study how the heart worked. "I remember concentrating very hard on learning that, more so than on anything else, because I thought it was so interesting. For a long time I wanted to be a physician. I liked a television show called *Quincy*, which was about a medical examiner."

Until she was 13 years old, Sue lived in Pennsauken, New Jersey, close to Philadelphia. She is the youngest of six kids. When she was 13 her family moved farther out from Philadelphia to a town called Medford. "In Pennsauken my five older brothers and sisters went to the same high school and we were thought of as sort of a dynasty in that school. When we moved I went to a different school and nobody knew me or my family. That was an interesting challenge, but a good one, because it made me rely on myself more and not on the fact that I was from this big family. It made me a little tougher because I went through this big change and moved out of the only town I had ever known. The town we moved to had a much better school district so my academic life was more challenging. I didn't work very hard in the 7th grade, but in the 8th grade I had to work hard and that snapped me out of

GROUNDBREAKERS

Inventor and Electrical Engineer

Edith Clarke (1883-1959) Edith Clarke studied math and astronomy at Vassar, then taught math at a private girls' school and a university. She later studied electrical engineering at MIT and earned the first master's degree in Science ever awarded to a woman from the electrical engineering department. While working at General Electric, she invented a "graphical calculator" that could be used in solving electric power transmission line problems. Later she became the first woman to teach electrical engineering at the University of Texas at Austin.

Source: The ADA Project (TAP) Past Notable Women of Computing

my malaise. I was always very independent after that. I played field hockey and softball and loved them both, and I was in student government and chorus in high school.

"My guidance counselor urged me to look at electrical engineering as a field difficult than any pre-med program. I regret listening to her and letting somebody else influence me that much, somebody who didn't know me that well and obviously didn't know what a pre-med major was compared to electrical engineering. But I'm not sorry I went into electrical engineer-

It's extremely important to find people you can rely on to guide and mentor you. Women are still a minority in science and technology. We have come a long way and are reducing a lot of barriers, but it is still a very isolating experience, because there are so few of us, so you need to find that network of support.

of study for college. She told me she didn't think my grades were good enough to do pre-med. In hindsight I think that is absolutely hilarious because my undergraduate education in electrical engineering was far more ing because it led me to biomedical engineering, and that has allowed me to understand the medical aspects of my work. I wouldn't want to be a doctor today. But I like working with applications that are important to medicine."

Sue went to college at Drexel University. During her first year she enjoyed her English course more than the science and math she had to take, but when she got to the point in school where she could take electrical engineering courses that involved design and not just theory and she could actually build things, she really started having fun. "That physical connection is very important to me."

In her senior year she took a series of courses in control systems and biomedical engineering. "Those are the two topic areas that I liked the most and still like the most. I learned in graduate school that your body is made up of lots of control systems that regulate it—the cardiovascular system, respiration, lymph system, nervous system—all these systems take information that helps the body decide whether the current state is a good one or whether adjustments need to be made."

During her undergraduate work at Drexel, Sue participated in a cooperative education program with the Navy. After she finished her degree, the Navy hired her as a civilian engineer and gave her a scholarship to graduate school at Rutgers in biomedical engineering. She studied and worked for the Navy when she didn't have classes and then went back to work for them full time once she had her master's degree. In Sue's field it's good to have a Ph.D., so she started her Ph.D. program at Rutgers after she finished her master's. She worked full time while she studied for her doctoral degree in biomedical engineering.

Her work at the Navy involved reviewing a lot of proposals for research that the Navy paid private companies to do, so she learned what to look for in a proposal. That has helped her write good proposals for funding today. Sue also worked on various projects involving computerized sensors. In one project she designed a sensor that determines what type of aircraft is about to land on the deck of an air carrier, so that the wires that stop the plane can be set at the right tension for that type of plane.

Begins Her Family

Sue played on a Navy women's softball league. Her coach was a man named Dennis, another Navy civilian engineer. Since she was one of the few women on the team who actually had experience playing softball Dennis noticed and appreciated her. The two dated and eventually married. When Sue got pregnant she quit work to have her son and then went back to work a few days a week. But when she got pregnant with her daughter, she and Dennis decided that she would stay home and take care of the kids.

After 14 months of not working, Sue decided she needed to work again and began looking for jobs in biomedical engineering. "I had a couple of different offers, but the firms were far away and would have required an hour or more commute in each direction. With the children being so little I couldn't see doing that; it would just add too much stress to my life. My husband, who had gotten a job with Lockheed Martin, put my resume in with a group called the Advanced Technology Labs at that company, and I got an interview with them. They were doing a lot of artificial intelligence work for the Department of Defense and also working on software systems using the mobile code technology. They made me an offer for a job and, even though it wasn't an area I was particularly interested in, there wasn't much of a learning curve because I knew how the DoD worked, and was familiar with the technology they were working with, from my work at the Navy.

"It was the path of least resistance, but it turned out to be a very nice job. I worked with a wonderful group of people who gave me time to get up to speed on their technology. I got to do a lot of fun design work and to help implement what we designed."

When she was working at Lockheed Martin, Sue went to Dartmouth to give presentations about her group's work more than once. Lockheed Martin was a subcontractor to Dartmouth on a project called ActComm, which involved the mobile code and mobile computing technologies. "I became friends with some of the people at Dartmouth, and when the Institute got funded they told me about it. Dennis and I had always wanted to move to a more rural area. It's incredibly beautiful here; this was the type of place we wanted to raise our family. I got asked to interview for a position, and it was wonderful that I got hired."

At first Sue and Dennis thought that Dennis should find an employer other than Dartmouth, because they didn't want both of their jobs to be dependent on the same organization, but Dennis had trouble finding his type of work at a company in New England so he chose to work at the college in a new technical area.

"Dartmouth is a great place to work. We are just in awe many days. We're able to do great research, we have a fantastic group of people to work with, and it's a very laid back atmosphere here. We both feel very fortunate to be here and raise our family in a great place like this."

Lisa Phifer

Lisa Phifer

Vice President, Core Competence, Chester Springs, PA

Major in Computer Science, master's degree in Computer
Science, Villanova University, Villanova, PA

Computer Network
Security Specialist

Tricks of the Wired and Wireless

Think of a computer network like a highway that connects your home with your school and the offices where your parents work, only using wires (and sometimes wireless technology) instead of streets. The Internet is a public computer network. It connects computers all over the world. There also are private computer networks owned by companies, governments, schools, and professional and industry associations. These networks make it possible for people working in different places to access information stored on the network in databases or other types of software. The networks can connect people as near as in the same building or as far away as in different countries.

Computer Security Consultant

Independent computer security consultants can earn more than $100,000 per year, but you have to be willing to work hard to promote yourself and bring in new business.

LISA'S CAREER PATH

Experiments in her
home chemistry
laboratory

Decides on
computer science
major in college

Interns at Unisys,
then goes to
work there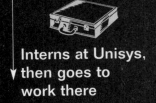

As a network security specialist, Lisa Phifer has to keep up with what's happening in the fields of computer networking and computer security. Her company, Core Competence, provides information about security products and tests products made to keep computer networks secure, so people who aren't supposed to have access to the information stored on the networks can't break into them. People who steal or destroy information they aren't supposed to see by breaking into computer networks are called hackers or attackers.

"One of the exciting things in my field is that people who don't know a lot about security are now becoming more aware of it," Lisa says. "For a long time network security was just sort of a necessary evil. People who developed and implemented computer networks in large companies were aware that they had to spend money on it, but they didn't see how they got a lot out of it. Now all sorts of people are starting to become aware of the need for security. People who have computers in their homes are switching from Internet telephone dial-up service to broadband access (where they are always online) and this exposes their computers to the attackers more. So they are becoming aware that they need personal firewalls—software that stops attackers from getting into your computer and probing around, finding files you left unprotected that they might want to damage for the fun of it or to get personal information."

Attends international standards meetings

Gets advanced degree at Villanova at night

Helps build North Carolina Information Highway at Bellcore

Lisa tests network security products to see how easy they are to use, how well they work, and what's the best way to install them. Computers in networks can be connected to each other either through wires or through wireless (radio) technology. Right now Lisa is most interested in products made for wireless networks, because many people are using devices like personal digital assistants, cell phones, and laptop computers that can employ wireless technology to access information stored on computer networks. Wireless networks are easier to eavesdrop on or to break into, so products that make wireless networks more secure are important to lots of people.

"We have a test network where we select a number of systems—pieces of networks, firewalls, routers, and other things used in networks. We put each product into this network to see how it actually performs. We want to find the product's pros and cons. There are a number of different ways to stop somebody from eavesdropping on a wireless connection, so we test out different ways of using the product to accomplish that goal and decide which we think is most user-friendly. Sometimes we are asked to test a product to see if it will withstand attack, but generally we focus on how usable the product is. If we are going to recommend to companies that they actually buy this product and put it on their network, we need to be able to explain what the impact on their network will be. Ideally you want security to be as transparent (invisible) to users as possible so they don't have to do a lot extra to have a secure connection."

Joins Core Competence, develops network security expertise

Writes book on wireless LANs

Writing a Big Part of Her Job

Lisa spends a lot of her time looking at products and providing the cations like *ISP Planet* (www.isp-planet.com), which provides news for Internet service providers, and sometimes for magazines that are printed. Last week Lisa and her

We have a test network where we select a number of systems—pieces of networks, firewalls, routers, and other things used in networks. We put each product into this network to see how it actually performs.

companies that sell the products with feedback about what the products do and don't do well and how they compare to other similar products on the market. She also writes about these products for publications, sometimes for Internet publi-

business partner David wrote an article for *Business Communications Review* about "network security best practices"—the things that companies should be doing to keep their networks secure. This list of "best practices" in computer security gave Lisa and David a chance to share their knowledge of the methods they see working well to protect information stored on computer networks.

"One of the things I really enjoy about my job is that I get to work with other people interested in the same topics and get to share ideas about what good technologies and practices are. I also really enjoy testing products and writing about new technology developments. I get paid to do the testing and the writing, but I'm also getting paid to learn, to watch for what's going on in the industry. If I see anything that looks new and interesting, I might be able to get paid to try it out.

"Because of the pace of change in the information technology industry everyone is releasing new software at a much faster pace and it's often more complex than in the past. Sometimes the software is not tested enough, so it's easier to find weaknesses in it that make it vulnerable to attacks. The Internet has helped hackers to learn

CAREER CHECKLIST ✓

You'll like this job if you ...

Won't be scared off by lots of detailed work, can pursue problems thoroughly

Want to continually learn, will keep studying computers

Can look for the big picture, as well as the details

Like to do "detective" work, are persistent and patient

Can work well with others

Love to write and will work to learn to be a good speaker

Can live with some uncertainty about your next paycheck

new tricks. They share their tactics on chat boards, bulletin boards, and e-mail lists."

To keep up with what's going on in the industry, Lisa subscribes to several newsletters about security issues. These newsletters come to her e-mail address every day with Internet "hot links" to information about companies that have new computer security or network products, new ways that hackers are finding to get at and/or destroy computer information, new computer viruses circulating throughout the Internet, and other security information. By knowing what types of attacks are occurring on computer networks, Lisa has information to help her evaluate which products are most useful to protect networks.

Lisa is the vice president and one of two owners of her company. The only other employee is the president, David. "We like doing the testing, consulting, training, and writing work more than the administrative work of running the company. When we need help, instead of hiring more full-time employees, we partner with other small companies that have the expertise we need." For example, Lisa and David wrote a report comparing different small router firewall devices a business could put in front of its small of-

"Our goal in writing the report was to help people understand what this category of products covered, what the different features were, and what products were on the market. We

It's really fun where I am. I have direct control over where my career is going.

fice computer network. Most of the companies that make these devices also have a Web server (a system that displays Web pages to users on the Internet) because the small companies that buy the products often want to put up their own websites. Lisa and David solicited the help of someone whose expertise was Web development and Web servers to evaluate the Web servers contained in the products they wrote about, since that isn't one of their areas of expertise. Core Competence published the report on its website (http://www.corecom.com) so that people interested in the topic can read it. Anyone who wants this report in the form of a paperback book can also order a copy through this website.

looked at dozens of products in summary, and eight different products in detail. We initially financed the report by charging the companies that we wrote about in detail a small fee for testing. When we put the report on our site we got a lot of 'traffic and hits' and we were invited to write summary articles in different publications."

Now Lisa is writing a book about wireless local area network (LAN) security. In her spare time she reviews network and security book chapters and book proposals for publishers. A publisher she regularly works with asked her to write this book on a topic of interest to a lot of information technology professionals. It probably will take six months to write, working on planes, as Lisa travels to give seminars or visit customers, and from home on the weekends.

Conference and Training Responsibilities

Another service Core Competence offers is a conference on network security called The Internet Security Conference (TISC), which is attended by people who are responsible for network security at their companies. Core Competence also develops content for other conferences. Right now Lisa is working to find experts for a series of panels on wireless networking security for an upcoming California conference on wireless technology. The conference organizers came to Lisa to create the conference sessions because they knew she was interested and knowledgeable about wireless network security and also because she has experience developing conference content. She has to decide what type of discussion would be most interesting and relevant for the people who attend the conference and then find the right people to talk at the session.

Lisa also speaks at conferences, and she gives training classes on networks and security at companies. She has traveled to Turkey and to China to give classes. One of the classes she teaches fairly frequently is on virtual private networks (VPNs). VPNs are a way of using a part of the Internet to create a computer environment that "feels private," even though it is using shared network resources. No one can access the VPN except the people who have the right passwords and security clearance. To keep that space secure, the VPN makes it extremely hard for others to eavesdrop on traffic sent over the Internet or to intercept or change information located there.

"The Internet is pretty much accessible anywhere so it tends to be easier to get to and cheaper than actually setting up private networks. VPNs are a growth area. People didn't know what VPNs were all about when we first started teaching about them and didn't understand the underlying technology but now they know something about the technology and are trying to get to the next level—how they can manage it better, make it more secure, reduce the overhead costs associated with it."

Lisa has worked with Core Competence's president, David, for her entire career, on and off. "He sat across the hall from me in my first job and we became friends. He decided to start Core Competence when he was working for Bell Communications Research in network consulting. He thought he could do the same kinds of things that he was doing at Bellcore independently and have a little more control over the type of work he did and whom he worked for, and also maybe be more richly rewarded.

"After he started the company I was talking to him about a project I was working on. I had to go to Arling-ton, Virginia, during the week and then come home to Pennsylvania on the weekends, and I mentioned to him that I had kind of had it with being away from home so much. He asked me to come and join his company as a consultant and part owner.

"My original hesitation was that I'm a technical person and not a marketing person. In a small company all the employees really have to market themselves and be on the lookout for new work. I wasn't sure I would be comfortable with that part of the job. But David is very good at promoting the company and since I was very strong technically, I thought it would be a good combination of skills. It's worked out to be a very good combination for us. I've also gotten more comfortable selling my skills to prospective clients."

Lisa has worked at Core Competence since 1995.

Thought She'd Become a Chemist

Growing up in Wilmington, Delaware, Lisa had a dad who was a chemist at DuPont. He thought Lisa was born to be a chemist, too. He used to bring home glassware from his laboratory for her to use in her chemistry lab. She enjoyed doing experiments, and she thought she would be a chemist when she grew up. The day she turned 16 she got a job in a chemical company. "I quickly figured out being a chemist wasn't quite what I thought it was going to be. It required a lot more exacting lab work and patience than I had pictured playing with my chemistry set."

Even though Lisa was pretty sure she didn't want to be a chemist, she continued to work at the chemistry company and was a chemistry major her first year in college at Penn State University. "I started looking at career alternatives because I knew chemistry might not be for me. I took a year off. Then I returned to school at West Chester State, where I spent a year majoring in English. But although I consider myself a good writer I'm not a creative writer and so I never thought of writing as a serious career path; I thought you had to be creative to make a living as a writer. I went through career counseling and the counseling tests always suggested that I should look at accounting or computer science or something to do with math. There was actually this one exercise that asked you to picture yourself at a party with different groups of people like accountants and computer scientists and see which group you would rather be with. I realized I didn't want to spend my time with accountants, and that's how I picked computer science as my major. After I took my first computer science course in college I was hooked. The problem-solving aspects of it appealed to me. That is what all the things I work on now have in common: you are presented with some type of challenge and the trick is to think of some way to meet the challenge."

During college Lisa worked at the chemical company managing the shipping department and doing computer data entry. When her work hours conflicted with her class hours she left the company to do odd jobs, like pumping gas and working on a construction crew, where she did dry walling. "I thought about being a tradesperson, but even though the work of the plumbers and electricians looked interesting, I couldn't see myself working outdoors when I got to be older."

The Right Place at the Right Time

In college Lisa interned at DuPont and then got an internship at the computer company Unisys. It was luck that she ended up in the network architecture part of the company. "I was in the right place at the right time. The Internet was just starting to be thought of; there wasn't really any firm concept of a large public network like the Internet when I started. I had the opportunity to work on many different aspects of network product development. I started by doing some debugging and testing of the products, and then I moved to the group that actually designed the networking protocols. Then I got moved into software development, coding the same things I had just designed. So I got to see the same products from several different perspectives, and that taught me an important lesson. I don't think if you just work on one facet of the product you have an appreciation for what's involved. Being able to follow the same product along its entire evolution was really enlightening."

Later, as part of her job, Lisa got to attend international meetings of computer experts who were trying to come up with standards for computer networks. Although the Internet networking standards already had been created by the U.S. Department of Defense, many people throughout the world thought there should be another standard for networks that was not military. So representatives from different companies met to discuss what that standard should be, although eventually the Internet protocols did become accepted throughout the world. At these standards meetings Lisa met people from many different types of computer companies, including employees from Bell Communications Research (Bellcore). While Unisys was a company that focused on the computer, Bellcore was a telephone company and so networks were even more important there.

Lisa eventually found a job at Bellcore working on networking projects that explored how telephone lines could be used for more than just voice conversations. One of her favorite projects was helping to build the North Carolina Information Highway, a high-speed public computer network designed to support applications such as distance learning and video-conferencing. College and high school instructors could use the network to teach students who weren't in the same physical location. Doctors at different hospitals could use the network to discuss cases with each other. Prisoners could be arraigned by judges without having to travel from the jail to the courtroom.

"After helping to design the network and to build it, my job was to go to North Carolina and work at the central offices, training network operators on how to get the new network up and running and to fix things that weren't working at first. This network was a new thing at the time and there was a lot of interest and excitement in it."

Lisa worked at Bellcore for four years on various network projects before she joined Core Competence. She started working toward her master's degree at Villanova night school right after she graduated from West Chester. It took her eight years to finish because she had to travel for work. Because Unisys and Bellcore provided tuition assistance, the challenge was not financial—it was just being in town every Monday and Wednesday night for 10 weeks in a row.

Lisa wasn't involved in network security until Core Competence, but she has now learned enough about it to be considered an expert in the field. "It's really fun where I am. I have direct control over where my career is going. It's very motivating to me to see the direct relationship between the efforts I expend, the success of the company, and the reward I get. It's also nice to have an impact and to see my work in print."

Lisa has lived with a friend and partner Judy for 14 years. In her spare time she and Judy like to travel. Some of their favorite vacations have been to Tahiti and Costa Rica. Lisa is a scuba diver and loves traveling anywhere the water is warm and clear.

GROUNDBREAKERS

Mathematician

Emmy Noether (1882-1935) A German mathematician credited with founding abstract Algebra, Emmy Noether audited classes in math at a German university before women were allowed to take them for credit. Later, after becoming recognized as an expert mathematician and lecturing in math at the university level, Noether helped Albert Einstein formulate his theory of relativity. Physicists remember Noether for Noether's Theorem, a foundation stone of quantum physics.

Source: Nobel Prize Women in Science

Jeri Richardson

Jeri Richardson

InfoSec Specialist, U.S. Department of the Treasury, Washington, D.C.

Major in Computer Science and Organizational Behavior

Federal Information
Systems Security Specialist

Assessing Risks and Securing Systems

Jeri Richardson's job is to make sure that information stored on the computers and the computer networks at the U.S. Department of the Treasury is secure. Jeri has to certify that the Treasury's computer systems are compliant with federal security regulations. To certify a computer system in the federal government is to perform security tests and identify vulnerabilities; then perform a cost/benefit analysis, determining which vulnerabilities should be eliminated and finding ways to reduce risks. The goal is to be sure that unauthorized individuals cannot access the information, and that the system has the necessary security safeguards in place to be sure the data is complete

Federal Computer Systems Security Specialist

Jobs in the federal government are paid by a system of grade and step, which is determined by the nature as well as the location of the work. Computer jobs usually start at about $25,000. With several years of service and increasing responsibility, some employees can move into computer security jobs that pay more than $100,000.

47

JERI'S CAREER PATH

Gets married
▼ young and has
three kids

Goes to work for the
▼ state of Maryland

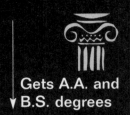

Gets A.A. and
▼ B.S. degrees

and unaltered and the system is available when needed.

The owner of the computer system (or system administrator, who is responsible for the system), the information systems security officer, and the computer users' representative all have to agree to what has to happen and be in partnership about how it will happen. "One of the things I like best about this work is that I get to interact with all different types of people—technical people and computer users as well as contractors. I like to talk and I have the ability to make people feel comfortable. I'm a people person.

"When I go in an office I tell them 'We're here to certify your system; we're going to do security testing in order to find the vulnerabilities of the system'. Then, I assure the system owners and the users that we are not attempting to crash the system. We're professionals and we are here to make sure that the data within the system is secure from unauthorized individuals. We're not here to destroy the data or try to blame anyone when we find vulnerabilities. I have to gain their trust or they won't talk to me. If I did not get the cooperation of the system owners and users, performing my job would be impossible.

"If you are doing your job and learning, you are going to make mistakes. So when a mistake occurs on a particular system because of something the system owner or user did, it's not an earth-shattering event. I tell people we can fix it. If they feel confident that they can come to me and say 'I did this and it didn't turn

Enters federal service
as secretary

Moves into computer
operations

Works as a
computer
programmer

out the way I thought it was going to, help me fix this', I can go in and straighten it out. That's the way I approach problems; the more information you can give me the faster we can resolve the problem." This type of attitude has always been important for Jeri to have but was particularly important when she worked on a computer help desk.

When Jeri is assigned a system to certify, she develops what's called a statement of work. This is a document that explains in detail what has to be done in order to make the system secure. Usually the work that needs to be done will include a risk assessment, penetration test, vulnerability assessment, and security test and

evaluation. Once the vulnerabilities are identified, a cost/benefits analysis is completed to determine the most cost-effective ways to eliminate the vulnerabilities. In some cases it is not cost-effective to correct the problems. Security plans specify what security mechanisms are in place, and then an action plan is developed to reduce the vulnerabilities. A security mechanism can be something as simple as a password a user must have to access the system or something as complicated as encryption software that will make it hard to read the information without the right "key" to unlock the data.

This statement of work is put into a request for proposal and sent to a number of private companies that work with the federal government to find a contractor who wants to perform the work. Jeri evaluates the contractors' proposals and selects the contractor best suited for the job. Then Jeri works with the company se-

It would have been a lot easier for me to go to college before I had kids. I would have been better prepared financially to care for my children, and that's what I try to explain to young people today.

lected to make sure that everything goes smoothly. She makes sure the contractor delivers what was promised and that the company gets paid on time. She also makes sure that the contractor employees have credentials to enter the building and access the system so they can assess system vulnerabilities and can test the system's security.

"I know how risk assessment is supposed to be done and how vulnerability assessment is supposed to be done. I am familiar with what is necessary to complete a security plan. I'm a go-between, managing the project, making sure the contractor does a thorough job in testing the system and locating all the vulnerabilities and that the contractor comes up with the most cost-effective ways to safeguard the system. When all that's

CAREER CHECKLIST ✓

You'll like this job if you ...

Can be very persuasive

Aren't afraid to say what's on your mind

Can talk in front of a group of people

Won't be intimidated by people who are high-ranking within the organization

Love to continue learning

Will be able to manage people and budgets well

Love to read

done I certify the system and state that it meets the federal regulations, that it has been tested and all the major vulnerabilities and risks have been addressed. Then I recommend that the system be accredited. A report goes to the designated accrediting authority (DAA), who makes a decision about whether the system should be accredited. The DAA ultimately is responsible for the system and for accepting the risk of operating the system, and he or she has to determine whether the residual (remaining) risks are at an acceptable level."

Looking at Vulnerabilities

"When we look at the vulnerabilities of the system, there is a whole list of things we have to consider. The vulnerabilities would belong to one of the following categories: physical, administrative, software, data, environmental, hardware, network, or Internet. For example, to assure physical security we want to assure that the network servers are housed in an area that can be secured, that we don't have people wandering in and out of that area unless they are authorized to use the system. We assess whether the perimeters of the system can be breached. Firewalls (that protect the system from being breached) and intrusion detection devices (that notify the system administrator when someone is trying to break into the system) are only two of the technical solutions we use.

"We develop a security architecture that includes strong passwords, firewalls, and other technical solutions to assure the security of the information that we process. We also have people on site (where the system is located) whom we can report to if we suspect a break-in. If we think the system has been broken into we have a team called the incident response team. They will investigate what has happened and correct the security problem.

"We may have different companies or contractors performing various tasks. There are contractors that are responsible for the day-to-day operation of the system, and then we have contractors who are responsible for installing security devices and monitoring security. I have to interact with all these people."

vulnerabilities. We then have a sense of all the vulnerabilities in the system. We identify the risks as high, medium, or low, and we address all the high-risk areas first. For example, if a computer server was located under a fire sprinkler, that would be high risk. We would want to move the server to a different location or get rid of the sprinkler immediately so that

You have to have technical skills and you can get them in college. College gives you the ability to know how to research information and how to think critically.

"When we are in the process of certifying a system, we require a test plan that shows how the contractors will test for the vulnerabilities. The contractor submits a test plan to the system owner and myself, and we review it. If we decide it is thorough, we go ahead and set a date for the testing. After the testing the contractor creates a report that identifies the

there would be no danger of water shorting out the server and causing the system to go down. We then create an action plan, listing all of the vulnerabilities with the corrective measures and dates for the work to be completed."

Cheap and Expensive Fixes

"We have to do a cost/benefit analysis of the risks. Some risks are very easy and cheap to fix, like using strong passwords. Others are more expensive. If you need to rewrite the application, for example, it might not be cost-effective to fix, especially if the risk is practically negligible. I make the initial determination of whether it's an acceptable risk and put the recommendation in the report that goes to the DAA. If the DAA feels that this is not an acceptable risk, then he will provide the funding to fix it."

Jeri has worked in many different aspects of information technology. She has been a computer operator on mainframe computers. She built computer networks using personal computers and computer servers. She has done troubleshooting and supported computer users by fixing their systems and computers when they break down. And she has worked on a computer help desk (users call this desk when they don't know how to do something on their computer and want step-by-step advice).

Grows Up in New York

Jeri grew up in New York City, an only child. Her father, who had a stroke when she was just a baby, stayed home and took care of her until she was seven. "I was always very comfortable being around men because of that. I was a tomboy—hung out with the guys and boxed, rode bicycles, played handball and basketball all the way through high school.

"In the early 1960s, when computers were these huge mainframes, I was about 15. I wanted to take a course in computers but my mother didn't believe that spending the money would be worthwhile. I got married and had three kids and dropped out of high school. My husband died and I had to raise the kids. When all my kids were in school and I was 26, I decided to go back to school."

Gets a Federal Job

While she was working for the Maryland state unemployment office, making determinations about whether people who filed for unemployment insurance benefits were eligible under the state's rules to receive these benefits, Jeri enrolled in Prince Georges Community College in Maryland to study computer science. She took at least one course every semester and went to summer school. As soon as she got her degree she got a job with the federal government. "I was trying to get into the computer field, but they wanted people with experience so I got a job as a secretary. That was the fastest and easiest way to get into the government."

While she worked full time during the day, Jeri attended college at night. Her first degree was from Prince Georges Community College in Computer Programming, with a certificate in Computer Operations. Then she got a degree from Columbia Union College in Maryland, where she majored in Organizational Behavior, a degree offered by the psychology department. Later she did graduate work in Management and Develop-

In the federal government there are many challenging careers in the computer field. Individuals with the appropriate technical skills can work in Web development, software development, network operation, network security, systems administration, database administration, and information systems security—to name only a few.

ment of Human Resources at National-Louis University.

Jeri worked for the Department of Housing and Urban Development and the Voice of America doing secretarial work. Then she got a job with the federal government's Department of the Interior in the procurement office. "I was responsible for small purchases like furniture, magazines, and books. I tracked those purchases in a database. One of the reasons they hired me was because they knew I could manipulate a database."

After getting some government work experience with computers, Jeri applied for and was accepted for a position at another federal government agency, the Defense Mapping Agency, as a computer operator. She had to input data into a mainframe computer by mounting tapes on to tape drives, putting punch cards into a card reader, and mounting huge disk packs into their drives. "In the old days, to program a computer you sat down at a keypunch machine and punched out cards that you fed into the card reader. Then they came up with terminals you could just type the program into, and if you had a problem you could go in and edit the program, which made it much easier. That's how you get information into a mainframe computer."

From the Defense Mapping Agency, Jeri moved to the Naval Audit Service, where she installed computers, configured software, networked computers into the Local Area Network (LAN), performed daily and weekly backup on a Wang mainframe computer, and provided technical support to the users.

"Every job I had prepared me for the next one. I built on each and every skill I learned and it all just flowed together. It was amazing. I think it was God's plan; it wasn't mine because I didn't have a plan."

Most times when Jeri moved to a new position she was given a pay increase and a promotion. "It's hard to get promoted if you stay in the same agency in the federal government, especially if you are a woman and you are black. Most of the people in IT (information technology) in the government are still men, although there are more women than there used to be."

From the Naval Audit Service, Jeri moved to the Pentagon, where she worked on classified computer networks and managed the help desk. Jeri landed a position at the federal Defense Information Systems Agency (DISA), where she was responsible for the integration of existing security systems, certification and accreditation of information systems, and development of new security products. "When I worked at DISA we were exposed to every security issue that came up. I traveled all over the world supporting users at different military bases."

Jeri then moved to the Treasury Department, where she is currently employed.

Keeping Up With the Field

Today Jeri keeps up with what's happening in the security field by checking the Internet for news about security vulnerabilities, reading computer periodicals, and keeping in touch with friends and colleagues who work in the computer field, which seems to be just about everyone she knows these days. "We'll e-mail each other when new security regulations come out or when there is a new threat we need to know about."

Jeri was in an auto accident last year and has trouble sitting, so her free time is usually spent at the gym in the whirlpool or the swimming pool. She is getting better, though, and she is grateful that her employer, the federal government, has made it easy for her to continue working. She also has a strong faith in God. "I am a Christian and I believe God has protected me and taught me and cared for me, and he continues to do that." Jeri is also very active in her church.

Alexis Slebodnick

Alexis Slebodnick

Senior Criminal Analyst, Customs Cyber Smuggling Center, U.S. Customs Department, Fairfax, VA

Major in Business, master's degree in International Transactions, George Mason University, Fairfax, VA

Cyber Smuggling
Analyst

Waging War on Pornography

As a girl, Alexis Slebodnick didn't dream she'd end up catching bad guys on the Internet. She was shy and bookish as a child and only interested in parties and clothes as a teenager. "No one who knew me thought I'd end up in a serious career."

But Alexis has spent 20 years in a serious, but fun, career as a criminal analyst for the federal government. It is hard to think of Alexis as anything but serious. In the "war room" of the U.S. Customs Cyber Smuggling Center in Fairfax, Virginia, Alexis works with four other analysts and dozens of special agents. She uses lots of computer technology to secure the Internet from crimes. As a senior analyst in the Child Exploitation division, Alexis's mission is to end child pornography on the Internet, which is believed to hold as many as

Intelligence Analyst

With a bachelor's degree, beginning analysts in the federal government earn about $30,000 and can earn as much as $119,000 as managers. The average is $65,000. Those who work in the private sector can earn more.

300,000 illegal images of children as young as two. "The bottom line is saving the kids."

Alexis spends hours combing through information and evidence, known as intelligence, gathered by special agents street addresses, and phone numbers on an individual case. Once she determines which pieces of evidence are credible, she sends them to Customs forensics experts who photograph all evidence and load it onto computers. That way the original evidence is protected by not being used re-

Alexis became the FBI's first representative to the Treasury Department's Financial Crimes Enforcement Network, which was created in the early 1990s to stop money crimes on the Internet.

who bring it in box loads to the center. Wearing gloves to protect herself and the evidence, Alexis searches through thousands of paper documents, computer disks, address books, and other materials looking for names, e-mail and peatedly. Alexis then organizes the information using her computer's "Analyst Notebook" software. The software allows her to make charts and graphs of evidence, which she uses in the case reports she writes and sends to field agents.

Marries Paul

FBI's first representative
to Financial Crimes
Enforcement Network

Master's degree
in International
Transactions

Alexis shares her analysis of a case with agents in the field offices. When all agree there is enough evidence to move forward with arrests, they prepare to meet in the war room to go over the case. For Alexis, that means giving a presentation on the intelligence she has analyzed. She uses the Cyber Smuggling Center's graphics room to make huge charts of information stored on her computer: the individuals in the suspected crime and their roles; the Internet sites they post on; the victims; dates that alleged crimes happened; and a sequence of events. Alexis presents the information to other Customs officials who sit around a long conference table. A flat monitoring screen called a "plasma screen" allows the people in one conference room to see others in a neighboring room. With the use of three desktop computers, Alexis can tap into the Internet

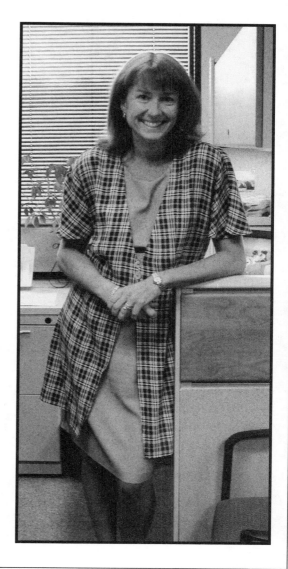

or the internal Customs Service software. A war room chalkboard also can be hooked into the computers so that information can be traded between it and the computers. As people shout out ideas and suggestions, notes taken on the chalkboard transfer to the computers. These can later be printed so everyone doesn't have to take notes. A detailed map of the United States allows Alexis to show with colored pushpins where crimes occurred.

Securing Information

Another part of Alexis's job is to analyze conversations in Internet chat rooms set up by agents to communicate "undercover" with child pornographers. The agents build their case by asking for pornography,

requesting types of children, and inquiring about prices. Alexis trains other analysts and agents, some of whom come on the job with no computer skills, to use various types of software and computer tools (like protective software called firewalls) to shield their identities when they talk to bad guys over the Internet. "The biggest thing about technology here is using it not only to catch criminals, but also to protect the analysts and agents. Part of my job is to help them stay anonymous."

Sometimes Alexis has to go to the suspect's Internet service provider (ISP) to obtain copies of his e-mail. If an ISP is based outside the United States, the Customs Department has to work with the foreign government to obtain the e-mails it needs. Alexis has to work with many foreign law enforcement officials. In one of her biggest cases, known as Operation Blue Orchid,

Alexis analyzed the Internet usage of a San Francisco man who bought hundreds of videos of Russian-made child pornography, then set up Internet chat rooms and forwarded requests for child pornography back to Russia. Customs agents got online and easily received information on buying the videos and where to send the money in Moscow. Agents used the money-wiring company Western Union to track the money back to Moscow. Of 22 suspects believed to be living in the U.S., so far 16 have been arrested and 11 have been convicted. This was possible because of close cooperation between U.S. and Russian officials.

Some criminals have been emboldened by the Internet, thinking they can remain anonymous online even while they advertise illegal items blatantly. "They're not too shy about what they do on the Internet because they think it's hard to track them." But the criminals are wrong. Even a cursory search of the words "child pornography" can yield hundreds of websites. Customs analysts have received more than 10,000 tips about Internet child pornography since January 2000, and believe that there are more than 100,000 websites mar-

CAREER CHECKLIST ✓

You'll like this job if you ...

Like to solve problems

Love to read and write

Are organized

Can juggle multiple projects and be flexible about changing priorities

Are curious and like to learn new things

Can communicate well and work with all types of people

Can work independently and as part of a team

keting child pornography. "We could never work them all. We just try to focus on the biggest and the worst."

Although her work can be disturbing, Alexis's work is also rewarding. "When people do get brought to justice, that is so great. And it's so exciting when it makes the evening news and I know the inside details. I feel like I've made an impact and done something important."

Sometimes Alexis's work can be tedious. Because pornography often is recycled, the Cyber Smuggling Center keeps a library of 860 magazines of child pornography to compare to images analysts find on the Internet. The comparisons allow them to determine whether a real child is currently being abused or whether an electronic image is taken from an old magazine picture. Alexis once worked with three other employees, eight hours per day for four months, to scan 21,500 pictures so the center would have electronic images of child pornography to compare to what could come across the Internet. Keeping track of old and new pictures has always been important in securing the Internet from

pornography. But it became critical in early 2002 when the U.S. Supreme Court ruled that police must prove that a picture is of a real child, rather than a composite, before making an arrest. "What started out as a digital library for our use has evolved into the National Child Victim Identification Program (NCVIP). The NCVIP is a multiagency initiative created to facilitate the identification of child pornography produced using real children. This is in response to a recent Supreme Court ruling (known as the Ashcroft decision)."

Being a criminal analyst also takes patience. One of Alexis's first cases when she began at the center in 1999 involved an Internet child pornography ring out of New York. After spending two years on the case—a length of time not uncommon—Alexis sent the file to an agent in New York City who finished the work. The case was ready to go to trial on Sept. 11, 2001, when the terrorist-driven jetliners struck the towers of the World Trade Center where the file was held. Luckily, her office in Virginia keeps paper and electronic copies of all cases, so the file was reconstructed.

Alexis's job is much like that of a special agent. She pieces together information to solve crimes and can even issue subpoenas for witnesses to testify about what they know about a suspect. "I do pretty much everything but carry a gun." The other difference between criminal analysts and agents is that analysts mostly stay in the office and keep regular daytime work hours. Agents, on the other hand, may get called out at all hours of the night to catch do each day, but I can never do them all. We stay so busy. I work on several different cases every day. It's the kind of job where you never get everything done and that's OK."

One of the reasons that is OK is because the Customs Department respects personal time and physical fitness. Alexis runs with co-workers every day on her lunch break as a stress reliever and to stay in

I work on several different cases every day. It's the kind of job where you never get everything done and that's OK.

criminals and can be put into very dangerous situations. Also, federal agents usually are relocated to different states every three or four years. Because of those differences, Alexis says she knows she chose the right career for her. Even with the steady hours and office work, there's never a dull moment.

"There's no typical day and that's good. We get five or six unexpected things, emergencies, every day. I make a list of things to shape. Even on their busiest days employees are encouraged to take exercise breaks to stay alert. And no matter how busy she gets, Alexis always leaves at the end of her eight-hour shift to care for her two "babies," black Labrador retrievers, Hunter and Lycos.

A Surprising Career

Alexis and her only sibling, Alison, who is two years younger, were born in Germany, where their father was stationed in the Air

I never expressed an interest in law enforcement and when I was in high school I just wanted to go out to parties and have fun all the time.

Force. The family moved to Springfield, Virginia, in the Washington, D.C. suburbs, when Alexis was five. Although a military family, Alexis's family stayed in Virginia rather than moving around as some military families do. Alexis and Alison stayed active with piano lessons, Girl Scouts, and family outings to museums and concerts.

"I enjoyed Scouts a lot, especially the camping trips. I also enjoyed earning badges because it was fun to learn new things and the competitive side of me liked to try to earn as many as I could."

Alexis graduated in 1981 with a bachelor's degree in Business from Radford University in Virginia. She hoped to follow in the footsteps of her aunt, a fashion merchandiser for a department store chain, who bought clothes—and received many as gifts—at New York fashion shows. "I loved clothes then and still love clothes!" But after being turned down for one department store job and realizing she'd have to work her way up as a clerk, Alexis decided to change her career goals. She returned to her hometown and saw an ad in *The Washington Post* about the FBI. Fascinated by the mystique of the agency, Alexis applied and was accepted after passing a written test and oral interview. However, a government hiring freeze kept her from getting a job. "I still don't know why they posted the ad."

Alexis decided to take a temporary administrative job at the Naval Research Laboratory, where she learned how to use computers and met her husband Paul. Two years later, and much to her surprise, the FBI hired Alexis and quickly appointed her as an analyst in its newly formed drug unit.

"This surprised everyone. No one ever thought I'd end up in law enforcement. And I never really thought I'd get on with the FBI. I never expressed an interest in law enforcement and when I was in high school I just wanted to go out to parties and have fun all the time."

But Alexis had qualities important to law enforcement that most people overlook. "I was good at getting people to talk to me. My supervisor didn't care what my degree was in. He thought a broad background was good and said just getting any bachelor's degree showed that I was smart and willing to learn."

Alexis soon became the FBI's first representative to the Treasury Department's Financial Crimes Enforcement Network, which was created in the early 1990s to stop money crimes on the Internet. She spent nine years at the network, learning various software programs such as Excel and PowerPoint, which also helped with one of her favorite hobbies, genealogy, the study of ancestors and family relationships. She earned her master's degree while assigned to the Financial Crimes En-

forcement Network. Since most of the money-laundering crimes investigated had an international aspect, Alexis thought that classes dealing with the International Monetary Fund, World Bank, and similar institutions would be beneficial. She ended up with a master's degree in International Transactions. Since some of the classes were applicable to her job, her employer paid for them.

It was Alexis's love of trying new things—and a short attention span—that took her in many directions in her career. "I've moved around a lot, but somehow I've always managed to be on the cutting edge of different things. I'm always looking for a new challenge." Alexis's next challenge will be as part of the Department of Homeland Security, which is taking over the Customs Service and many other agencies.

After 20 years in the government, Alexis now enjoys five weeks of vacation per year, which she and her husband spend camping and traveling to beaches and national parks.

Sandra L. Lawrence

Sandra L. Lawrence

Computer Security Engineer, Defense Information Systems Agency, Washington, D.C.

Major in Physical Education; master's degree in Health Education, Adelphi University; Adelphi, NY; master's degree in Information Technology Systems, George Mason University, Fairfax, VA

Military Computer
Security Engineer

Keeping the Navy Safe

Commander Sandra Lawrence has had to handle many aspects of computer security in her 22-year Navy career. Today her job is to engineer security into software products used by the U.S. military in the Global Command and Control System (GCCS). The GCCS is the computer system that keeps track of U.S. military troop movements and supplies throughout the world. One project the GCCS supports is Operation Enduring Freedom, President Bush's initiative to combat terrorism and terrorists.

Sandy works for the Defense Information Systems Agency to assure that all software products incorporated into GCCS won't compromise the system's security.

Navy Computer Security Engineer

In the Navy and all branches of the U.S. military, pay is dependent upon rank and years in service. Promotions depend on performance and time in service. Basic pay constitutes the greatest portion of most service members' paychecks. Basic pay starts at about $964.80 a month for enlisted personnel with less than four months' service and tops out at about $11,737.20 a month for four-star officers with at least 26 years in uniform. Navy personnel get a housing allowance and free medical and dental insurance for themselves and their families, and money to attend school and obtain technical training.

Software developers create products to help the military move troops more efficiently, like databases that predict when certain kinds of supplies should be reordered and "what if" scenarios that help military leaders determine the best place to put troops to achieve military objectives.

"I have to know the current federal government and Department of Defense computer security requirements. I have to keep learning all the time, to keep current about the latest threats to security—like new computer viruses or threats from intrusion to the system (hackers)—and I have to understand what the future security protections will be, so we can begin to implement them into GCCS.

"I and other security engineers at GCCS get information from the National Security Agency and other federal agencies that deal with computer threats. We want to learn what threats are out there that might affect what we do here at GCCS. We look at what the National Security Agency recommends and what the Department of Defense says are the vulnerabilities we need to be most aware of. Then we analyze that information and ask, does this affect the GCCS, and if so, how can we engineer security to protect against those vulnerabilities?

"We take that information and decide what security posture we should have for the future—say five years out—and then we build our policies and procedures to support that vision.

Joins Navy/Assistant
▼ Security Officer

Teaches at National
▼ Defense University/gets
another master's degree

Naval Space
▼ Command/London
assignment

We look at what other organizations are doing that makes the most sense for us, and we incorporate those practices that will work well for us into our own security practices."

For example, Sandy has to know what new computer viruses have been created and how to create and send updates to the software that will protect the system against those viruses. There are about 600 GCCS computer servers and 10,000 GCCS computer workstations around the world that have to receive the updates.

Works With Developers

Sandy also meets with developers of new GCCS software to make sure they are building security into their products. "We have to give them guidance—say 'you can't do this' or 'you must do this' early in the process. We can't wait until the end when they deliver the software and then say 'you didn't do this and now the product can't be sent to the field because it is a security risk.' Getting our software developers the right guidance is a big deal. We have to take the policies of the Department of Defense regarding security—for example, encrypting information in a certain way to make it secure when it's sent through our computer system—and figure out how to incorporate those policies into our day-to-day work."

Sometimes GCCS will buy commercial "off-the-shelf" products such as word processing software. Then Sandy's group has to figure out how to

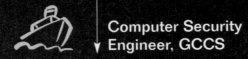

Goes to sea

Computer Security
Engineer, GCCS

Getting our software developers the right guidance is a big deal. We have to take the policies of the Department of Defense regarding security—for example, encrypting information in a certain way to make it secure when it's sent through our computer system—and figure out how to incorporate those policies into our day-to-day work.

assure that the commercial products can be used securely within GCCS. Often security in commercial software products is weak so a "security fix" for the software is necessary.

Creates Users' Guide

Sandy's group creates testing materials developers can use to test software for security weaknesses. "We also invented a security users' guide that shows developers what security we will expect with each new release of a software product. We meet with developers to advise them what security features the Department of Defense and the National Security Agency want to see in our software. We work with a lot of contractors and I have to make sure they are delivering what they have agreed to deliver to us."

Sandy and her colleagues often go to conferences that GCCS users and developers attend to brief them on what GCCS is doing in terms of security. GCCS security engineers work closely with the security officers at military sites throughout the world, communicating by e-mail, fax, and telephone, to inform site security officers about GCCS security policies and the actions GCCS is taking to make the system secure. Sandy and the other security engineers have to make sure that when GCCS sends a new product out everything works right and that, when it sends out updates to fix security problems, installing the updates doesn't cause other problems for the system's users.

Sandy administers a budget of $2.5 million, which she uses to pay those who work for her at GCCS and contractors who build security into the software products.

CAREER CHECKLIST ✓

You'll like this job if you ...

Work well with different types of people

Can be articulate and will be able to explain and defend your decisions

Will learn computer operations and how computers work

Will continue learning all the time

Are logical, will be able to deduce the source of a computer problem

Think you could manage other people and budgets well

Every new piece of software that is put on GCCS has to be certified and accredited. Representatives from the National Security Agency test the software's security through a variety of methods and show where there are any problems or holes in it. GCCS security engineers then review the problems and develop a plan to mitigate or fix them. All of this information goes to the Joint Chiefs of Staff Directorate for Command, Control, Communications, and Computer Systems to accredit the software—in other words, to take responsibility for it by saying they understand and accept any security risks associated with the software sent to the field.

Sandy's days are filled with writing updates to software, meetings, briefings, and e-mails. "We update computer files daily, answer queries from developers and site security officers, go the conferences to brief on security and to meetings to brief developers, check to make sure contractors are doing what they said they would, and make sure the certification and accreditation process goes smoothly.

"We're always interacting with other agencies. Every group has its own agenda; everybody hates the security engineer. The developers hate us because we make their lives hard, the users hate us because we have to change their passwords and send out updates frequently to keep the system secure, the approving authorities and the Department of Defense hate us because they think we should be this way, figure out a game plan'. You have to be a realist in this job.

"You also have to understand computer operations and be able to figure out why something isn't working. We had a problem that took us weeks to figure out. We thought it was a hardware problem but it turned out to be the software. You just have to keep trying things until you find the solu-

Joining the military was not something my family or my friends on Long Island did. It was totally unexpected for me to do it.

doing more for security. It's always a balancing act. To do this job, you really have to be able to work well with all types of people. That's the first and most important requirement. You can't hide in the back. You have to be able to defend your actions. You also have to be logical. When you say 'You can't do this' you have to explain why and then offer a way to mitigate the situation—say, 'maybe we can do it tion. You have to break things down logically. You also must understand who gets the data from GCCS. This can be a tough problem. If you send data to one person and it gets mixed with something else from somebody else, what wasn't a security risk before can now become a security risk and all of a sudden the information is classified. The fact that everybody is so interconnected these days makes our job harder."

Loves Sports

Sandy never thought she would end up in a computer security career. As a girl growing up on Long Island, in New York, there were no computers in her schools. She loved sports and played field hockey and tennis all the way through college. She boated with her family in the summertime. They went crabbing and clamming in the Great South Bay off Long Island. Her main interests in high school were physical education and health. When it came time to go to college she went to Nassau Community College and obtained an associate's degree and then to the State University of New York at Cortland, where she majored in Physical Education. She picked Cortland because it had one of the top phys ed programs in the country at the time.

Sandy loved school and went on to get a master's degree at Adelphi University in Garden City, New York, in Health Education while teaching phys ed and coaching in high school for four years. "In New York, you got a temporary teaching certificate and then you had five years to get a master's degree so you could get a permanent teaching certificate. Adelphi gave me a scholarship because I did so well in my undergraduate work. I taught, coached, went to grad school, and played field hockey and lacrosse on the weekends. I was living at home so it was easier to balance all these different activities because I didn't have to cook and do laundry."

Joins the Navy

Eventually, Sandy became dissatisfied with teaching because it didn't seem to be a secure career. There were too many teachers in those days and not enough jobs. "The schools would let you teach four years and then let you go. They would find somebody else they could hire for less money, because after five years you had tenure, they had to pay you more, and it was much harder to lose your job."

It was the early 1980s and the Navy was building up its fleet of ships to fight the Cold War with the Soviet Union. Sandy signed up for Navy Officer Candidate School one summer, thinking the Navy would offer a secure career and she could work in a health program like drug or alcohol rehabilitation. "Joining the military was not something my family or my friends on Long Island did. It was totally unexpected for me to do it." But Sandy knew the Navy needed more women. It was sending more men to sea. Although federal law prohibited women from being assigned to ships, they were needed for shore jobs in communications, administration, and computer jobs that men left to go to sea.

There weren't as many Navy jobs in health as Sandy had hoped. So she elected to get a computer job. After her officer training she got assigned to the Navy Yard in Washington, D.C., working on a top-secret computer system called the Worldwide Military Command and Control System (WMCCS). "It was a big mainframe with its own communications system that was the forerunner of GCCS."

Her first job was assistant security officer, a job for which she needed a top-secret clearance, which she got easily enough because there was nothing bad in her background that would prevent her from getting it. But she also needed basic computer knowledge, which she didn't have. The Navy sent her to school to learn about computers. Sandy studied programming and computer operations.

In her job she was responsible for putting in user identifications so people could access the computer system, regularly changing users' passwords, and reading the computer audit logs to see if they showed any activity of someone trying to break into the system. She had to review software code when the programmers changed something to make sure there were no security problems with the changes. When the system crashed she had to be able to read the report in computer language to see what had happened and how to get the system up and running again.

The Navy used to move people around to different types of jobs throughout their careers. It was likely Sandy would be transferred to a job outside the computer field after she finished her first assignment. To stay in the same specialty was unusual, especially early in a Navy career. But in Sandy's case, all her jobs ended up being in computer work! Her second job was at the National Defense University in Washington, DC, teaching computer science. By this time microcomputers, also know as personal computers, had been introduced and Sandy taught a course for middle managers to understand how PCs could be incorporated into their work area. This was a very popular course and she traveled all over the world. She also went to George Mason University in Fairfax, Virginia, to get another master's degree, this time in Information Systems Technology.

For her next assignment, Sandy landed at the Naval Space Command in Dahlgren, Virginia, where she was the computer operations officer with five people working for her. She was responsible for putting in the Command's first classified Local Area Network (LAN), a system that strung together all the Command's personal computers with computer servers. Classified command LANs were new at the time and Sandy had to learn how to make the system, which was secret, secure. Part of her job was to do a risk assessment for security risks. For example, she had to estimate the probability that a plane taking off from the base air strip would crash into the building and destroy the computer system, or that the servers would be damaged by water, or that someone could read the information on the computers from across the street through highly sensitive antennae.

Sandy had to analyze what the biggest risks were—were they the loss of the information, the loss of software, or the destruction of hardware?—and develop a plan to address those risks. She had to quantify the dollar amount those risks would cost and then decide how best to protect the system and the information. "There are books that tell you how to do all these things and federal agencies offer guidance. A lot of it you learn by experience."

GROUNDBREAKERS

Early Programmer

Grace Hopper (1906-1992) As a young Navy lieutenant assigned to the Bureau of Ship Computation Project at Harvard University, Grace Hopper programmed an early calculating machine that was called the forerunner of the modern computer At the end of her career she created sophisticated software programs for computers. She is credited with co-inventing the computer language COBOL.

Source: Prominent Women of the 20th Century

At Naval Space Command one of the biggest problems the computer operations people experienced was that the users didn't really know how to use the system and they were always "breaking" it. So Sandy wrote a users' manual to show people how to access the system properly.

Moves to London

Sandy's next assignment was in London, England, where she took over as department head for U.S. Naval Forces, Europe WWMCCS. She had 70 people working for her, including computer operations and computer security personnel. She took over the department four days before the beginning of Desert Shield, President Bush Sr.'s campaign against Iraq's invasion of Kuwait. She and those who operated the WWMCCS experienced a tremendous surge in the use of the system after the war started. It was important to make sure the system didn't crash. "If there is denial of service this is a security issue, because you can't get to the information you need to make decisions about how to fight the enemy. Our training increased by about 200 percent after Desert Shield began."

From London, Sandy was transferred back to Washington where her branch provided technical database support to 22 WWMCCS database systems throughout the world. Then she was sent to the Middle Eastern country of Bahrain, as the computer operations and security officer, supporting more than 100 people assigned to U.S. Naval Forces, Central Command and Fifth Fleet. Her computer systems were critical in the planning and execution of bombing missions against Iraq in November 1996.

She got her first assignment aboard a ship just after the Navy permitted women to go to sea on combatant ships. Sandy spent two years aboard the USS Nimitz as its first Combat Systems Officer, in charge of 200 enlisted personnel and 10 officers who were responsible for the ship's computer systems, including operations and security. Sandy and those who worked under her were responsible for three separate LANs, two classified and one unclassified, with more than 800 servers and workstations. The advent of the Internet made everything about securing computer systems more difficult. Sandy's group was responsible for the ship's three websites; for assuring that sailors, who had access to the Internet aboard the ship, didn't visit pornographic or hate-related websites; and for monitoring sites to see that sailors didn't give away information about the ship's movements in Internet chat groups. All this was in addition to maintaining all radar and satellites, all communication systems, one of the ship's weapon systems, all electronic display systems, and two TV network systems. Sandy and her crew were a very busy bunch. "It was usually at least an 18-hour day. The ship was the most arduous tour I had because of the hours and setting up a whole new department and learning how to be at sea. It was pretty intense, but I'm glad I did it."

These days when Sandy isn't working, she's probably taking classes. She is studying for a certification in Systems Engineering. She does find some time to have a little fun—playing golf, gardening, and volunteering at a local computer club for girls.

Rosemary J. Erickson

Rosemary J. Erickson

Owner, Athena Research, San Diego, CA

Major in Psychology; master's degree in Sociology, San Diego
State University; San Diego, CA.; Ph.D., Sociology and Justice,
American University, Washington, D.C.

Security Consultant

and Author

Sociologist Turned Security Expert

Dr. Rosemary Erickson believes the best way to secure, or protect, a place is by understanding the people who threaten it. Rosemary has spent more than 30 years as a sociologist, someone who studies people's behavior. Her understanding of people, especially criminals, allows her to consult, or instruct, others on how to stay safe from crime.

"I don't try to solve crimes. I try to prevent them by understanding crime, training people, and making physical changes," says Rosemary, a consultant and author on physical security. Unlike securing the Internet, physical security is about keeping people and places safe.

Security Consultant
Typical pay rates for security consultants are $250 per hour or $2,000 per day. Salaries can go well over $100,000, especially when working as an expert witness.

ROSEMARY'S CAREER PATH

Rosemary has made her career first by studying crime and criminals, then by training people to avoid becoming victims. She has written dozens of reports and articles and produced videos to share her information with companies and with the federal government. She has taught many companies how to be safe, and she often serves in court as an expert witness in court on security.

As a consultant, Rosemary works on many different projects at any one time. Working out of her home office near the beach in San Diego, California, she usually starts her day on the telephone, either responding to requests for media interviews about her work or scheduling appointments. Many of Rosemary's media contacts, and even some lawyers who hire her as an expert witness, have contacted

My dad and mother were the major influences in my life. My gender was never an issue regarding what I could and couldn't do or what my aspirations should be. My parents never discouraged me, nor did they push me in any particular direction.

her after finding her website, http://www.AthenaResearch.com, through search engines using the words "security" and "convenience stores."

Rosemary's workdays always include writing—either for research papers, presentations, or publications—and usually Internet research for crime statistics and other information. Many days also include investigations where Rosemary must travel to places where crimes have occurred to study how a business might have prevented the crime through better security. She travels all over the country. Sometimes she interviews people, such as convicted felons and security managers. On other days Rosemary develops security-training programs for businesses, or she travels to court-

rooms to testify or give depositions—hours-long discussions about what she found in an investigation—as an expert witness.

Rosemary estimates that she spends most of her time in three activities: one-third on research, one-third on training, and the other third on expert witnessing. She also spends some time with the media, teaching and giving presentations. The work stays interesting because she handles many different projects. "I'm always working on at least ten unrelated things at once."

Rosemary's claim to fame as a security expert happened more than ten years into her career. In 1975 she was part of a famous study, funded by the U.S. Justice Department, on how to make convenience stores, such as 7-Eleven, safe from crime. Rosemary was in charge of studying data. Her husband, a social psychologist, the late Dr. Bud Crow, was in charge of managing the project. The couple recommended changes that have since

for less obstructed viewing; and training employees not to resist a robber.

"We were able to take that information and begin working with 5,000 7-Eleven stores. Our study is often referred to as a landmark study and

I don't try to solve crimes. I try to prevent them by understanding crime, training people, and making physical changes.

been common in convenience stores for more than 20 years: keeping little cash in the registers; posting signs about the stores having little cash; using height markers by doors so clerks can give better descriptions of how tall robbers are; using good lighting; keeping posters out of windows

it's the best example of using research findings. It's where I saw the biggest result of my work."

Rosemary says her security expertise stems from her sociology background. But her interest in people began long before she studied sociol-

CAREER CHECKLIST ✓

You'll like this job if you ...

- Are curious
- Like to tell people what to do
- Like to make sense of things
- Love to travel
- Enjoy writing
- Like to help people
- Can speak to many different types of people

ogy, when she was a young child and saw few people nearby.

Grows Up on a Farm

Born in rural South Dakota in 1942, Rosemary grew up on a farm that had no electricity or running water until she was six years old. The experience left her with memories that will last a lifetime, such as blowing out kerosene lamps every night and going out into the cold, dark night to use the bathroom. "You always remember going outside to the bathroom."

With her only siblings—two brothers—five and ten years older and the closest neighbors two miles away, Rosemary had limited contact with people, but that didn't stop her from

being interested in them. When she was five, Rosemary's parents got a telephone that operated on a "party line." Common in rural areas through the 1970s, party lines used a single circuit to connect several households to one telephone line. On the party line, young Rosemary could climb onto a chair, pick up the receiver, and listen to her neighbors' conversations.

"I think that started my interest in people. Everyone had a distinctive (unique) ring, so I knew when someone was getting a call."

Rosemary believes her upbringing was more "personal" than how many children are raised today. "Our big event was on Wednesday and Saturday nights when we went to the little nearby town of a hundred people and watched people come and go. That was entertainment. People used to just stop by the farm. No one called ahead. It was completely different from what we see now. TV, phones, and computers have really changed the way we interact. I had fewer forms of communication, but it made me interested in people."

Rosemary's schooling was also different—and she believes in some ways better—than what many children have today. She attended a one-room school from first through fifth grades. "The country school helped me because you hear everything that's being taught" to everyone. Rosemary was reminded of what she learned in past years and had advance notice of what she would be taught later. There were only five pupils at the school when she was in fifth grade. Then Rosemary transferred to a town school with 23 pupils for the sixth grade only.

When she was 14, Rosemary's father left the farm and moved the family to San Diego, California, a city of some 200,000 people at the time. There were 700 students in her freshman high school class. "It was a hard adjustment." Eventually she came to like the city and became an honor student at her new school. But, after only a couple of years, Rosemary's family moved back to South Dakota.

Again, Rosemary made the best of the situation. She was an honor student, became a cheerleader, and dated a football player. When it came time to choose a college, Rosemary thought she wanted to go back to California. She applied to San Francisco State University, which was a haven for the beatnik movement. But she changed her mind and decided to stay in South Dakota after her friends and family threw her a huge farewell party. Rosemary went to Augustana College, a tiny Lutheran school in Sioux Falls, South Dakota, which had a very different environment from the more radical San Francisco State. She graduated with a bachelor's degree in Psychology in 1964. The Lutheran Church was a strict influence in her life throughout childhood and college. "There was no smoking, no dancing, no drinking, and girls had an early curfew. They were determined we wouldn't have fun."

Breaking Barriers

Few career doors were open to women in the 1960s. Many people assumed that most women who went to college would become teachers or secretaries. Rosemary decided to minor in Business—"to cover my tracks." But she was fortunate that her parents allowed her to choose her own career.

If you go into business for yourself, you are going to work more hours—they'll just be more flexible. You're going to have to work the hours or you're not going to get paid. There are no benefits like paid days off.

"My dad and mother were the major influences in my life. My gender was never an issue regarding what I could and couldn't do or what my aspirations should be. My parents never discouraged me, nor did they push me in any particular direction."

After college, Rosemary took a state health department job in South Dakota that involved traveling to various mental hospitals. The experience taught her what she did not want to do. "It was too over the top for me to think of dealing with the mentally ill."

Rosemary then headed back to San Diego where she spent a year as a research assistant with the city's Community Welfare Council. She considered psychological research but quickly learned that she did not want any job that involved touching lab rats.

Her third job proved to be the best yet. In 1966, Rosemary became a research associate at Western Behavioral Sciences Institute in La Jolla,

California. "It was one of those glorious times in history when the government was funding research for social problems. We had about 50 employees—anthropologists, sociologists, and psychologists. We really felt like we were going to make a difference on the war on poverty," a social movement made famous by President Lyndon Johnson.

It wasn't unusual for Rosemary to spend three years working on a study, as she did in evaluating "the war on poverty," researching stepfathers and the mental health of their children and studying low-income people. Her work forced her to interview many people. Sometimes one study required thousands of interviews. Before long, Rosemary began managing research and supervised the work of as many as 30 interviewers. "I liked designing the questions and training them to go out and analyze the data."

Many exciting things happened to Rosemary during her 13 years at the institute. In 1969, she married the boss, Dr. Bud Crow, who was director of the Institute and a professor at San Diego State University where she had received her master's degree in Sociology in 1971. It was also at the Institute that Rosemary began studying crime and criminals, which launched her career into security. Some of her research titles there included "The Offender Looks at His Own Needs," "Utilizing Ex-Offender Resources in Rehabilitation," and "Robbery Deterrence: An Applied Behavioral Science Demonstration."

Rosemary's last major study at the Institute was her acclaimed work, with Bud, to improve security at convenience stores. Using 7-Eleven stores for experiments, the couple helped 7-Eleven lower store robberies by 30 percent. It didn't take long for all 7-Eleven stores and nearly all chain retail stores to take their advice. The result: Convenience store robberies are down 65 percent since the late 1970s.

From Analyst to Entrepreneur

The success of the convenience stores study and the loss of government funding for research projects led Rosemary and Bud to start their own consulting business, Athena Research Corporation, in 1979. Together the couple built their research and consulting work for private companies, which took over funding from the government in the 1980s. Rosemary liked the work, especially because private companies, which had more resources, were more likely to be able to implement her advice.

In 1989, Rosemary suffered a huge loss when Bud, her husband and mentor of 20 years, died from lung cancer. She pressed on, however, as the president of Athena Research, a position Bud had insisted on for her from the beginning, and grew the company throughout the 1990s. Athena clients have included Burger King; Chevron, Exxon, Mobil and Texaco gas stations; Hilton, Marriott, and Embassy Suites hotels; banks; grocery stores; hospitals; and security guard services.

Rosemary also added to her work by becoming an expert witness. Qualified as an expert witness in 16 states, she often testifies in trials in which someone, usually an employee or customer, has gotten hurt or killed because of a security breach.

In 1990, Rosemary married Arnie Stenseth, whom she had known in college in the 1960s. The couple lived in the Washington, D.C., area where Arnie was an actor and Rosemary continued her work with Athena, while teaching at American University. She received her Ph.D. in Sociology and Justice from A.U. in 1994.

Now Rosemary and Arnie live in San Diego, near the beach, and Rosemary runs Athena out of their home, while teaching sociology at San Diego State University. With her marriage to Arnie, Rosemary inherited two stepdaughters and their children, "so I became a grandparent without ever being a parent."

Rosemary enjoys her work, maybe too much. She admits she does not have a good balance between her work and personal life. But when she's not working, she enjoys gardening, walking on the beach, and playing the piano. However, she works 50-60 hours per week, which she accepts as the price for enjoying the flexibility of self-employment.

"If you go into business for yourself, you are going to work more hours—they'll just be more flexible. You're going to have to work the hours or you're not going to get paid. There are no benefits like paid days off."

Although Rosemary enjoys being self-employed, she is thankful that she was an employee for 15 years before she had her own business. "Working alone in your own company can be very lonely. If you've never had a work-group experience, you miss a unique phenomenon of co-workers, supervisors, and working with people under you. That would be a shame to miss in your life."

Rosemary has written extensively in her 35-year career, including a dozen journal articles and four books. She has also been the subject or expert in hundreds of media reports, including the *Wall Street Journal, New York Times, Los Angeles Times*, CNN, CBS News, NBC Dateline, Court TV, and MSNBC.

Roberta Bragg
Roberta Bragg

Owner, Have Computer Will Travel, Inc., Grain Valley, Missouri

Major in Biomedical Communications; graduate work in Computer Science, University of Missouri, Columbia, MO

Computer Security
Entrepreneur

Evangelist

Roberta Bragg is a "computer security evangelist." Roberta, who runs her own company, has shaped her career as a specialist on computer security for the Microsoft Windows operating system family. She travels all over the country teaching security, providing technical expertise during computer security audits, helping clients who need to install hardware or software to make their systems more secure, and visiting conferences and trade shows where she can learn about the latest developments in the security field. She spends a good portion of her time reading books, researching on the Internet all aspects of information systems, and installing and securing systems in

Computer Consultant
Independent computer consultants can make more than $100,000 a year, depending on education, experience, expertise, and how hard they work. However, many make much less and beginners always make less just starting out.

test and production environments. She also writes articles and books. Currently she is working on a book about how to prepare to take a Microsoft exam on making computer networks secure.

Roberta's company is called Have Computer Will Travel, Inc. She offers her clients security consulting, security assessments, technical training, and technical support. "The majority of my work is on the evangelism side. I have very few consulting engagements where I spend a lengthy period of time with one particular customer. I'd rather do the knowledge transfer or come in and be the technical expert on an audit that may have been going on for several weeks. I'll come in for a day or two."

Roberta has helped to design security curricula. As an adjunct faculty member of Seattle Pacific University she developed instruction on security for Windows 2000. Her company now offers her recently developed three-day Security Academy.

Because Roberta is an expert in her field, a lot of people send her questions by e-mail or call her up and ask how to fix a particular security problem. "But one of the things I like best about my job is

Gets job with
▼ computer consultant

Starts own
▼ computer company

Works toward
▼ graduate degree in
Computer Science

having somebody call or e-mail me and tell me that some work that I did, an article I wrote that appeared on the Internet or in a book, or that a question I answered in a conference seminar saved their bacon—that they tried it out on their computer network and they didn't get hit by the latest Internet worm (virus), or that some attack on their system was not successful because they followed the instructions that I gave them. Everybody likes to hear that they saved somebody else's bacon. It's fulfilling to have an impact."

Creates Her Own Niche

As Roberta was shaping her career as a consultant, she looked for opportunities to become an expert in areas of computing that not too many people were experts in and to provide information others weren't providing. "I had been a computer programmer for many

The majority of my work is on the evangelism side.

I have very few consulting engagements where

I spend a lengthy period of time with one

particular customer.

years and I had been doing Windows network administration. Working in that area, I noticed there was not a lot of information about securing Windows systems. I went to a couple of conferences where the emphasis was on Unix (another operating system) and mainframe computer security. The conference presenters and organizers did not seem to understand the Windows systems and had very little information on how to secure them. So it looked like an area where there was a great need and I began research in that area.

"In the computer science field it's extremely difficult to keep up. What you have to do is pick an area you are good at and like to work in and focus there. You'll never keep up with everything so you just do the best job you can. There is a wealth of information on the Internet now and it's a marvelous research tool. I also spend a lot of money going to conferences and I read everybody and everything.

"People who are employed by companies to do computer security should spend part of their time doing research. If you are employed by somebody else, you have the ability to go to conferences and your employer pays for it, but because I work for myself I

Consults and writes books and magazine articles

You'll like this job if you ...

don't get paid for the time I spend researching. That means I have to be more careful balancing my paid work with my research than someone who doesn't work for herself."

Roberta has owned her own company since 1991, but she worked as an employee for other companies to gain needed experience. She also went back to school after she started her own company and studied computer science.

Can look at complex things and take complex jobs to fruition

Can think things through logically

Like to find out how things work

Are good at communicating and have empathy for others

Will have the drive to run your own business and find clients

Like to read and write

Won't mind continuously learning to find the latest information

Getting Computer Experience

During the 1990s Roberta worked in various types of computer jobs to hone her skills. She taught programming language and was the head of the computer science department at Brown Mackie College in Overland Park, Kansas.

Roberta also taught programming at a computer school that catered to businesses. She worked for a seminar company that produced technical seminars on Microsoft products. And she was a systems administrator at a consulting company, where she also helped some clients to set up computer networks.

Today Roberta has her own clients all over the country and keeps her name in front of the information technology world by writing for different computer publications, among them the *Microsoft Certified Professional Magazine* and *SearchWin2000*, an Internet publication for Microsoft network security professionals. Roberta also has given Webcasts—live online presentations where people get online and ask questions of the presenter by typing on their keyboard. In July 2002 Roberta designed, planned, produced, and participated in the first Windows Security Summit. As part of this conference, a complete Windows 2000 network was made secure and placed on the Internet. Because the network was heavily publicized prior to the conference, many hackers tried to break into it, but none were successful.

One of Roberta's books is a guide to studying for the CISSP certification. That stands for Certified Information Systems Security Professional, a certification that about 10,000 people who have advanced knowledge in computer security have earned. "When I obtained the certification

One of the things I like best about my job is having somebody call or e-mail me and tell me that some work that I did, an article I wrote that appeared on the Internet or in a book, or that a question I answered in a conference seminar saved their bacon.

I could see there wasn't a lot of information about how to prepare for the exam. So I approached my publisher about doing a book. I did some of the research and had several other authors work on the book too. This book is a nice guide to computer security. It's meant to give you a broad-based background in different areas."

Loves to Read and Wants to Write

Roberta grew up in New England. Her high school computer education was limited to one session with computers in a math class. She loved English and science. Dissecting a frog was fun, but the most enjoyable times were reading novels, the classics as well as science fiction. She always knew she'd be a writer when she grew up. Her first publication was in high school, an article on music for *Teen Beat* magazine.

Roberta went to Missouri to college and met her husband there. The couple lived in Corinth, Mississippi in the 1980s. They had two small children. Roberta worked in sales, selling business forms, labels, and later computers. She had to travel hundreds of miles a day. One day she was having lunch with a client. It was a bad day for her and she told the client that for a nickel she'd find another job. He rolled a nickel across the table and asked her if she would like to work for him. He was a computer consultant, back in the days when computers were slow and expensive and only large companies could afford them. Roberta began working for him and learned a lot about computers. After a while she started her own business in Corinth, doing computer programming for companies and helping them with technical support.

"It was a good opportunity for me at the time because I had two small children whom I was able to take to work with me. I would bring the children down to the office where there was an extra room with a bed, TV, and toys. Sometimes when I had a deadline I would stay there and work all night. I'd take the youngest child, who was not in school yet, into the break room at the client's, where he was fawned over by all the employees of the organization. I approached clients with this idea in mind—sometimes I would bring my child with me. It would be much harder to do today, but because my skills were in demand and the businesses in Corinth were family-friendly, I could do it back then."

When Roberta and her husband moved to Missouri, she went to work for other organizations to get more computer experience, but she always kept her own company, knowing that someday she wanted to work for herself again, and sometimes providing computer consulting or technical expertise to a small number of clients.

Today Roberta lives in a little town near Kansas City, although she could live just about anywhere and do what she does. "I could live on one coast or the other and my clients would be a lot closer, but I like it here and it's relatively easy to fly to either coast. I think that in the future more people will do what I do— that is, work for themselves and use technology to communicate with people all over the world."

When she isn't working, Roberta likes to weave. She recently built a 60-inch 24-heddle loom. She has worked for many years doing tablet weaving and other small-loom weaving. A dream she has had for a long time is to retire and weave blankets.

GROUNDBREAKERS

Mathematician

Ada Lovelace (1815-1852) The daughter of Lord Byron, the English poet, Ada Lovelace was a mathematical genius who designed her own method for automatically repeating the steps to produce complex calculations. Lovelace is known as the first computer programmer, and the U.S. Department of Defense named a universal standard computer language called ADA in her honor.

Source: Prominent Women of the 20th Century

Kristen Lloyd

Kristen Lloyd

Mechanical Engineer, Cepheid, Sunnyvale, California

Major in Mechanical Engineering

Mechanical
Engineer

Fighting a Deadly Bacteria

"**I** figured out at a young age the excitement of taking something apart and fixing it," says Kristen Lloyd, referring to a TV her mother was going to throw away because she thought it was broken. Kristen figured out how to fix the TV and discovered how satisfying that feeling was. She didn't know then that she would make a career of designing and fixing equipment that would be important to people all around the world.

Kristen is a mechanical engineer. She has designed and tested equipment that detects anthrax, a deadly bacteria. Kristen worked on anthrax-detection equipment as an employee at Cepheid, a bioengineering company in Sunnyvale, California. Now a student in a doctoral program for bio-

Mechanical Engineer in Biotechnology Field

You can start at about $50,000 and go to $100,000 within 10 years with a bachelor's degree. Mid-career people can make in the mid-$100,000s. However, salaries fluctuate with the economy and where an employee works. Kristen's salary nearly doubled in four years, as was common in Silicon Valley in the 1990s, but less so now. Pay in this industry is supplemented by incentives such as licensing fees for patents that an employee receives for inventions.

KRISTEN'S CAREER PATH

Gets scholarships
to Bucknell
University

Plays basketball
in college

B.S. degree,
Mechanical
Engineering

engineering at the University of Washington, when she finishes her degree, Kristen will be a specialist in using engineering in health and medicine—something she began at Cepheid.

"We used cutting-edge technology to figure out things that most people haven't even thought of yet and we used them in altruistic (charitable) ways," Kristen says. "I felt like I could really make a difference. I believe in the things Cepheid does."

Kristen's first project at Cepheid was to work on a contract for the federal government involving an instrument the size of a desk—known as "MIDAS"—that used the DNA of microorganisms to determine whether they were deadly pathogens, such as anthrax, plague, or smallpox. It was the first instrument of its kind. Kristen's job was to make it work with fluids like water and blood. There were other instruments that detected pathogens by using lasers to compare spores, but MIDAS was the first machine to use all the steps that usually are done in labs—cleaning, processing, then detecting substances—analyzing DNA to determine if a microorganism were a deadly pathogen. "There are a lot of ways terrorists can fool us by using spores that look like anthrax. But, if you use DNA as a method of detection, you're 99.9999 percent sure if it's anthrax."

For all its successes, MIDAS had definite limitations. Kristen and others found design flaws in the instrument. They quickly worked to get

Goes to work at
▼ Cepheid in Silicon
Valley

Improves anthrax-
▼ detection instrument
to test DNA

Helps develop
▼ three better instruments
for pathogen detection

another government contract for an instrument known as "MIDAS II," which was much smaller and used newer technology for opening anthrax spores to get to the DNA. MIDAS II, however, was still not as good as Kristen and her co-workers wished. They soon invented another system, called ADS, which led to the current model for pathogen detection, the "GeneXpert." This latest instrument is a small, portable system that uses detachable components, or modules, to do every aspect of pathogen detection using DNA.

Kristen and others saw the invention of the GeneXpert as a way to expand business for Cepheid, a small company that began in the mid-1990s. Because it is portable and has detachable modules, the military can keep the instrument in war zones, or wherever troops are stationed, to quickly detect whether soldiers have been exposed to anthrax or other pathogens. The process is as easy as taking a nasal swab from a person, testing the swab in the GeneXpert, and, if a pathogen is detected, quickly giving the person an antibiotic. The instrument also has other uses very different from biological warfare. In the medical industry, it could be used to detect sexually transmitted diseases or Group B Streptococcus, a serious bacteria that can be passed from a pregnant woman to her newborn child.

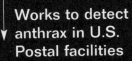
Teaches Postal Employees

The U.S. Postal Service currently is using the GeneXpert in a pilot project to detect anthrax. Post offices and mail sorting centers were among several buildings contaminated with anthrax in the fall of 2001 when someone mailed letters containing this deadly substance. The anthrax-letter crimes, which killed five people, really pushed Cepheid to find some answers. "If you'd asked us a year ago if we could have a system in a pilot atmosphere and be testing this many

I really wasn't interested in going to a big company where some engineers stay anchored to their desks for years. I knew I would have to have opportunities to relate more to other people in what I was doing. I wanted something cutting-edge and exciting. I decided that Silicon Valley was the place to be.

systems, we would have said 'absolutely not'." For six months, beginning in December 2001, Kristen flew from her company's headquarters in California to Washington, D.C. every month to show the Postal Service what the GeneXpert could do. Although the contract put pressure on Cepheid, it also put pressure on the Postal Service to change its ideas about an important aspect of the detection systems—the use of disposable parts in machines. While some in the government viewed disposables as wasteful and expensive, Kristen and others worked to convince them that the use of reusable parts was not worth the risk of having microorganisms contaminate letters or other items that did not originally have anthrax.

CAREER CHECKLIST ✓

You'll like this job if you ...

Like to fix things

Enjoy math and science

Will study multiple sciences

Like to work with others

Are fascinated with how things work

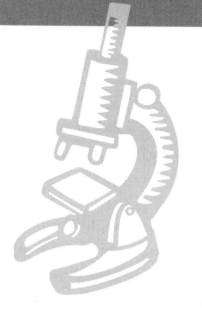

What would be perfect is if, in the next ten years, I would get my Ph.D. and do the research I feel passionate about. Then, pull some people together to do another start-up.

Cepheid began work on anthrax detection more than three years before the terrorist plane crashes of September 11, 2001 and subsequent anthrax letter attacks that captured the attention of people all over the United States. "When terrorism became Americans' No. 1 concern that year, I was comforted by the fact that I knew there were a lot of ways to detect terrorism and help. The government did have the forethought to know this was on the horizon. I answered a lot of questions for my friends and family because I'd been working on this for a long time. I knew a lot about it. It takes a really high dose of anthrax to be lethal. It's not like smallpox; it can't be spread between people."

For Kristen, a typical day on the job included time at a desk doing analysis and writing reports; time in the lab conducting tests and fixing instruments; and time working with other employees in the software and biology departments. Kristen worked hard at Cepheid, but her hours were flexible, based on what needed to be done rather than a 9-to-5 arrangement. "We pushed each other very hard and I worked until 10 at night sometimes. But that's not common. We were encouraged by flexible hours or gift certificates to restaurants or game tickets."

Decides on Engineering

Mechanical engineers can design almost anything from bridges to medical equipment. "I began researching my career options at the age of 11," Kristen says. "I asked my mother what the best jobs in the world were and she spoke of the traditional occupations: doctor, lawyer, and engineer. I never liked blood and I wasn't good at writing, so I ruled out the first two. I had no idea what an engineer was, so I looked it up in the encyclopedia." After reading about the endless things that engineers design, Kristen was hooked. "I described what I learned to my mother and assured her that I would definitely be an engineer."

Kristen, who grew up in Ellicott City, Maryland, also knew that she wanted a career where she could earn plenty of money. Her father, a high school English teacher, and her mother, a nurse, divorced when she was 11. As the oldest of four children, Kristen sometimes worried whether her mother had enough money. "I remember Mom always saying we had to be tight with money. So, I started thinking, What could I do that would make money?"

Although Kristen sometimes questioned her abilities to pursue a career in mechanical engineering—till a very male-dominated field—her high school math teacher encouraged her. "He said 'Math is your strong suit. You should definitely go toward mechanical engineering because it's so versatile and a great use of math skills'. That gave me the confidence to say 'Yes, I'm going to at least try it'."

Kristen chose Bucknell University, a private school in Pennsylvania, to pursue her bachelor's degree because it was a leader in using computer-aided design in

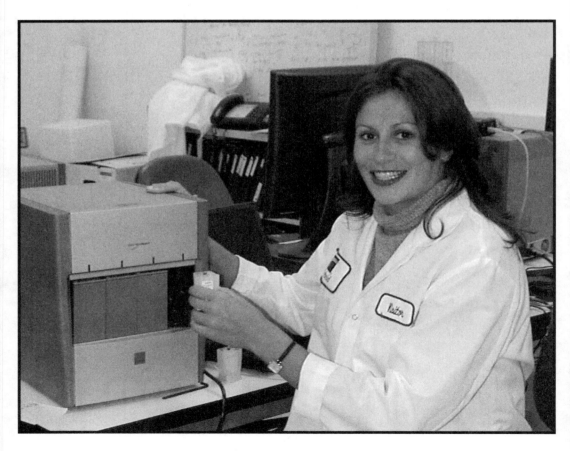

mechanical engineering. Smart, as well as athletic (she played basketball, softball, and volleyball in high school), Kristen received both academic and sports scholarships and played basketball all four years of college.

At six feet tall and as one of the few girls in her classes, Kristen says sports kept her from being self-conscious. "I think I can hold my own. That comes from playing sports—even pick-up basketball—and the coaches encouraged me to play as much as I could. My basketball coach said 'You don't have to be the best on the court, but you can always be the hardest-working'."

Kristen used her time in college to figure out which parts of mechanical engineering she liked and didn't like and where she might like to work after she graduated. "I really wasn't interested in going to a big company where some engineers stay anchored to their desks for years. I knew I would have to have opportunities to relate more to other people in what I was doing. I wanted something cutting-edge and exciting. I decided that Silicon Valley was the place to be."

The area just south of San Francisco became famous in the 1980s and 1990s for fast-growing and successful computer companies, known as "start-ups." Silicon Valley in the 1990s was also a great place for start-up mechanical engineering and biotechnology companies. One component of silicon technology is micro-machining (creating small devices). Micro-machining devices such as microfluidic "chips" give a small platform for analyzing biological samples and are sometimes referred to as "DNA chips." "Computer technology is related to the new ways of micro-machining and all sorts of silicon products. The same technology used to make computer chips (with silicon as the main ingredient) makes DNA chips."

Although she sent resumes to numerous companies in California, Cepheid was the only place that gave Kristen a call back without saying "Call us when you get to California." Cepheid flew her out for an interview and she was immediately impressed: the company was new and small and quickly filling with young, ambitious people like herself. She was hired as its 33rd employee. "That was the same number as my basketball jersey in college. I knew there was fate involved!"

As Kristen suspected, working at the small company gave her the information and skills she needed to broaden her mechanical engineering career. She also learned about business—targeting products and marketing for increased profits, the difference between government and private contracts, and the workings of biotechnology. "I loved the fact that I knew everyone and everyone knew me. You learn so much in that kind of setting. All of a sudden, I was working with all these brilliant people and learning so much and enjoying learning."

Dreams of Her Own Company

That great experience set Kristen on a new path. Because Cepheid rekindled her interest in biology, she is following through on her goal of getting an advanced degree, with the hopes of someday starting her own biotechnology company. "Going back to school is a personal goal for me. I want a broad background. I want to take more biochemistry courses and understand fundamental biochemistry issues." As much as she enjoyed the business side of her industry, Kristen also wants to expand her research in a college setting where profits are not the driving factor. "What would be perfect is if, in the next ten years, I would get my Ph.D. and do the research I feel passionate about. Then, pull some people together to do another start-up. If I have the ambition to start a company, which I do, I'll need the experience, education, and dedication to go to a venture capitalist [someone who lends money to new businesses] to get that money. I think a higher degree will help show my dedication."

GROUNDBREAKERS

Industrial Engineer
Lillian Moeller Gilbreth (1878-1972)

An industrial engineer and psychologist, Lillian Moeller Gilbreth worked with her husband Frank to develop time and motion studies of workers. Her book, *Psychology of Management*, was a classic text for scientific management. She also applied her industrial management techniques to home economics and the creation of devices and techniques to improve the lives of people with disabilities. She was immortalized in the book *Cheaper by the Dozen*, written by two of her 12 children.

Source: Extraordinary Women Scientists

P.J. Varrassi

P.J. Varrassi

Logical Security Analyst, American Airlines, Fort Worth, TX

Major in Psychology

Corporate Security
Analyst

Policy Maker

P.J. Varrassi is in a career field where change is happening at a faster and faster pace. As a logical security analyst for American Airlines, P.J. is a member of a team that must figure out any security threats to the company's computer system and develop plans for how to stop those threats. Logical security (security for computer systems) has changed as quickly as computer technology since the field became popular in the 1970s. Add to that constantly changing security threats and you have a whirlwind career. P.J. has spent more than 20 years in the field.

"What I like most about my career is that it is forever changing. When I first entered the information security field, very few people were in it. Having been on this career path for so

Logical Security Analyst
Usually starts with salaries in the mid-$40,000 range, and reaches the high $60,000s with several years of experience.

P.J.'S CAREER PATH

Psychology
▼ major, U of
Cincinnati

Relocates to
▼ Houston, hired
by MCI

Marries Bill
▼ and moves to
Dallas

long, it has been interesting to see the changes in technology and attitudes regarding security. Computer threats have increased and security has become more complicated. The terrorist attacks of September 11, 2001, forever changed the way people think about security—both logical and physical security. Who knows how it's going to be in the future."

Many more people are focused on security and there are many specialists doing specific security-related tasks. Companies have groups of employees called corporate security, who focus on physical security and terrorism: logical security to prevent computer security violations; security analysts—such as P.J.—assigned to study company policies and procedures related to security; privacy officers to make sure policies don't infringe on people's privacy; and lawyers to monitor all of it.

"The most important aspect in the field now is for everyone to be able to work together. To be effective in computer security, you cannot be an island. You have to understand everything: law, rights, ethics."

One of the most common security issues companies deal with is whether they can hold a person responsible for security breaches if the person didn't know he or she committed a violation. P.J. advises her company to explain all the rules of computer security to new employees their first day on the job. "That's so everyone knows the ground rules— basic stuff, like don't share passwords or access." Like company lawyers, P.J. advises her company on ways to keep the company out of trouble if security

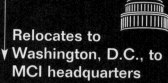

is breached. Explaining the rules to employees helps prevent the company from being held responsible, or liable, in a lawsuit.

"Too often, employees and contractors are given excessive rights where they can see things they shouldn't be seeing. If you've got a disgruntled employee, that gives you a liability."

P.J. spent 20 years of her career as a computer security technician or a consultant. In those jobs, she spent much of her time keying in user identification numbers and making access changes to computers. Now, as a security analyst, she works mostly on special projects, like reviewing corporate policies and procedures and computer access and working with internal auditors to determine who is certified to access what. P.J.'s goal is to prevent hackers or internal breaches that can lead to corporate espionage or other threats.

The Internet boom in the 1990s allowed people throughout the world to tap into a company's website, increasing security concerns, particularly those involving corporate espionage

P.J.'S CAREER PATH

| Supervises security staff at Worldspan | Does consulting | American Airlines security analyst |

P.J. studies what happens at her company that affects security and how security can be improved. In a typical day she spends most of her time attending meetings, working with different business units, or offices, and discussing ongoing projects by phone and e-mail.

P.J. gets assignments that often involve reviewing computer access or company policies. She meets with others who may be involved in her projects and she finds out, first-hand, what needs to be done to satisfy members of different business units within the company. "Sometimes things work well in theory, then fall apart in practical use." By meeting with other employees, P.J. can be more confident everyone will use her security plans properly.

P.J. stays in touch with many people by phone and e-mail to carry out her special projects and also to understand new developments in computer security. Although many aspects of the field change frequently, such as technology and security threats, the basic principles of protecting a company's information technology remains.

"The great thing about this field is that the principles are the same. You still have the same goals, but the software packages are different."

Security Used to be Easier

P.J.'s first computer job in the mid-1970s was before the popularity of personal computers—an invention that allowed anyone to have a computer on their desk. P.J. was an editing clerk and keypunch operator for a marketing research firm in Cincinnati while she was in college. Because few office workers had access to computers, there was less concern about security. When employees wanted something to go into the company computer system, they wrote it on paper and gave it to P.J. to keypunch onto cards, which would be fed into the computer.

"Everything was done on 11x14-inch pieces of paper. That's what you keypunched off of. It was very labor intensive."

P.J. worked on a large, central computer, which other terminals were connected to, known as a mainframe computer system and still used in some companies today. Using early computer languages such as COBOL, FORTRAN, and Pascal that have mostly gone the way of the typewriter, computer and systems programmers told the computer what to do to get the job done.

With so little access to company computers, there was not much interest in security and it was easier to control. A computer worker usually

CAREER CHECKLIST ✓

You'll like this job if you ...

Would enjoy communicating with many different types of people

Like to organize and track projects

Like both technical and non-technical types of projects

Will study to have a broad knowledge of technology

Would enjoy juggling multiple tasks

had multiple responsibilities that might include programming, troubleshooting, and security. That changed with the growth of the personal computer industry in the 1980s, which brought wide access to computers by workers throughout the company. The Internet boom in the 1990s allowed people throughout the world to tap into a company's website, increasing security concerns, particularly those involving corporate espionage (when company secrets are stolen to benefit a competitor). Then came September 11, 2001, when terrorists attacked the World Trade Center in New York and the Pentagon in Arlington, Virginia. "Now everyone is more concerned about computer security."

One of the biggest changes in computer systems over the years has been the decreased use of mainframe systems and the increase of personal computers. That change was hard for security analysts like P.J. who find the mainframes easier to protect from threats such as hackers. Personal computers connected to servers can easily be removed and stolen whereas mainframes cannot be picked up and taken somewhere.

"But mainframes are not going to go away totally. They're too much a part of some organizations." They are still the primary computer systems for certain information processing companies like credit cards and credit information bureaus.

Too often, employees and contractors are given excessive rights where they can see things they shouldn't be seeing. If you've got a disgruntled employee, that gives you a liability.

From Health Care to Computers

P.J.'s career in computer security came about largely by accident. She grew up in suburban Cincinnati, Ohio in the 1960s with one brother and two parents who both worked full time. She attended public schools and, not enjoying school much, decided to graduate high school in three years by attending summer school. She enrolled in the University of Cincinnati, planning for a health care career, such as occupational therapy.

"I wanted to really focus on teaching people to live within their physical restraints. My dad had had a few strokes and heart attacks and bypass surgery, so I was getting first-hand experience at home."

P.J.'s favorite subject was Psychology and she ended up with an associate's degree in Sociology/Psychology and a bachelor's in Psychology. She stayed at the university for graduate school and completed all the required courses for a master's degree in Education. However, before she had written her final thesis, required for graduation, she decided to enter the workforce. It was the mid-1970s and the economy was slow in her native Ohio, as well as in much of the country. She decided to move to Houston, Texas, where the oil and gas industries were booming.

P.J. took several administrative jobs in Houston before finally landing a job with MCI, a long distance telephone company. She was responsible for tracking problems with, and dispatching service for, a new MCI service called ADVANTAGE, which was attached to a company's phone lines to automatically route calls in the most efficient manner.

P.J. worked for MCI only a few months before she met and married her husband, Bill, an employee trainer based in Dallas. She relocated to Dallas after they were married. Bill was soon transferred to San Francisco. The only position MCI had for P.J. in San Francisco was an administrative job in its newly created information technology department. "As luck would have it, I had a certain knack for it. I enjoyed it. Security, to me, is very interesting."

Also lucky was the fact that P.J. had worked in security before as a security guard in department stores in Cincinnati while she was still in school. Although her security guard work focused on physical rather than logical security, "The principles are the same; only the method is different."

It didn't take long before MCI made P.J. the security administrator for its Pacific Region. She was quickly promoted to project manager, dealing only in computer security at MCI's headquarters in the Washington, DC area. Her task was to protect MCI's dial-up network, the means by which users access the MCI computer system.

In 1987, P.J. changed jobs and relocated to St. Mary's, Georgia, where she became a supervisor of the logical security staff for a military subcontractor, providing logical security support and auditing user identifications.

In 1988, P.J. went to work for Worldspan, which provides travel reservation services to Delta Airlines and Northwest Airlines. Again, P.J. supervised the security staff, looking for potential computer security problems and checking employees' permission to access certain parts of the computer system and their user identifications.

P.J. stayed in the job seven years before working as an independent contractor, then worked for a year at Equifax Information Systems in Atlanta, then again as a contractor. She landed the analyst position with American Airlines in 2000. She has lived and worked in the Dallas area since that time. "I really enjoy the people I work with. They've made this place great. American is the best company I've worked for. We are like family."

P.J. appreciates that, as a security analyst, she mostly works regular hours, allowing her time with her husband and 13-year-old son Christopher. Bill is currently retired from the United States Air Force and from jobs in corporate America. He spent 30 years in the telecommunications industry. The telecommunications industry was an easy industry to get a job in and Bill was able to follow P.J. to each new work location and get a job there without difficulty.

Raises Clydesdales

P.J. now has time to pursue a hobby she's dreamed of since childhood—raising horses. She and her family raise Clydesdale horses on their property outside of Dallas, which includes a 102-year-old house and 3,000-square-foot barn.

"I always wanted to own a horse. I was drawn to the Clydesdales because of their looks mostly. They are the St. Bernards of the horse family, having a gentle nature and willingness to work and please. They're made for strength, not speed." The average Clydesdale stands six feet at its shoulder blades and weighs 1,800 pounds. "It really does hurt when they step on your feet."

Getting Started On
Your Own Career Path

WHAT TO DO NOW

To help you prepare for a career in cybersecurity or national safety, the women interviewed for this book recommend things you can do now, while you are still in school.

JERI RICHARDSON, FEDERAL COMPUTER SECURITY SPECIALIST

Take all of the math classes that you can, because you will need good math skills to do many computer jobs. Get comfortable talking to people. In my jobs, I've had to brief very high-level people, including directors of agencies, generals, admirals, and the deputy secretary of defense. You can't be afraid of people in this type of job.

Plan to get a bachelor's degree and a master's degree. We are at a point where everything is in computers or networks. So it is important to have technical skills; you need a good background in computers. Also try to get into a work-study or internship program while you are in school, because employers seek individuals who have work experience and a degree.

MANDY ANDRESS, SECURITY MANAGER

Do a lot of learning and studying about computers on your own. That's what they are looking for in security managers and directors. So show a lot of initiative now. For information technology security you need a basic understanding of how technology works and what the default configurations for software and operating systems are.

Take any computer classes the school offers to get exposure to computers. Take a programming class. Down the road, it may be a requirement to have a master's degree in information security if you want to be a security director.

LISA PHIFER, COMPUTER NETWORK SECURITY SPECIALIST

Find a mentor—a teacher or parent who helps with the computer education program in your school—and learn all you can from that person. Explore computer security careers on the Internet.

SUE MCGRATH, COMBAT CASUALTY CARE AND EMERGENCY RESPONSE RESEARCHER

If you think you might be interested in biomedical research, first figure out whether you like math and science. Read magazines like *Scientific American*, which are written in easy-to-understand terms, to see if you are interested in scientific concepts and the research work being done today. Go to a hospital and ask if you can observe the instruments being used, especially how the MRI and CT scan machines work. Observe surgery to get first-hand knowledge of what surgeons do. Talk to somebody who is a biomedical engineer to see what the work is like. Do research on the Internet on different colleges, medical centers, and research institutions to find the type of work that would interest you. Then e-mail the people who are doing this work to see if they will explain more about what they are doing, or ask if you can "shadow" them for a day to get an idea of what the work is really like. Read biographies of women in science and those who have made major contributions to their fields of technology and science.

Some careers are very glamorous from the outside but on a daily basis they aren't very exciting. There are parts of every job that aren't glamorous and you should understand what these are and see if you can tolerate these duties. For example, when I worked for the Navy and for Lockheed Martin I had to fill out time sheets to account for how my time was spent. This often could be stressful because you have to remember every little thing you did that day. At Dartmouth I work more hours but there is a certain flexibility to the work which makes it easier.

ROSEMARY J. ERICKSON, SECURITY CONSULTANT AND AUTHOR

Read anything and everything about society and learn everything you can. Learn to write well. Plan to go to college and graduate school. Be interested in life and all the people around you. Watch the news and learn about current events and read the newspaper. Talk to your school counselor. Observe and keep an open mind about all people.

ROBERTA BRAGG, COMPUTER SECURITY ENTREPRENEUR

A good place to start exploring a career in computer security would be to find out what your particular school does in the way of security. Most schools now have people who are responsible for that. Ask them how they prevent a thief from getting into the grades at the school and how they protect the students from Internet fraud. Find out if there is a computer security awareness curriculum at your school or in your community.

You don't necessarily have to be good at math to be a good computer person. If you want to do certain things like write computer programs that will take spaceships to the moon you need to have good math skills. But there are other careers that require computer skills but do not require math expertise. In computer security there are a wide range of careers. You could be involved on the technical side or on the people side. On the people side, for example, you could be responsible for writing computer security policies and for that you would have to understand how computers work and how people work and be able to express yourself well. Whether or not you think you are interested in this career area, you need some knowledge of computer security these days because computers are becoming part of our world. You need to know how to protect yourself on the Internet and how to make sure no one invades your privacy.

ALEXIS SLEBODNICK, CYBER SMUGGLING ANALYST

Be active and get as many experiences as you can. Definitely get involved in sports or clubs. The more experience you have, even with things like the Girl Scouts, the more you learn to work together as a team to solve problems and be self-reliant. It gives you a broad view of what the world is like.

SANDRA L. LAWRENCE, COMPUTER SECURITY ENGINEER

Get as much knowledge of computers as you can, including learning a programming language. Do not try to become a hacker if you want to work in computer security. It will ruin your chances to work with any company that has contracts with the Department of Defense and many computer companies do. There are many jobs as computer security consultants in industries like banking and health care, so the outlook for this type of job is bright.

Read *The Cuckoo's Egg* by Clifford Stoll to get a sense of how one man tracked down hackers trying to breach a computer security system.

KRISTEN LLOYD, MECHANICAL ENGINEER

First of all, believe that you can be an engineer. Many people are intimidated by the term "engineering" and expect it to be a really difficult profession. However, if you are dedicated and believe that you can do it, you'll succeed. Challenge yourself to excel in the field of your choice.

Start asking questions now and learn as much as you can from other professionals. It's important to learn what people like about their job. You spend a large part of your life in the workforce, so you want to be sure that you're doing something you enjoy.

The Internet is an amazing resource that I would encourage all young people to use to their advantage. You can search for information on any topic and it is really easy to learn more about technology and engineering. I recommend searching university websites and reading about the research projects current students are working on. I find inspiration and learn about new ideas from reading about research by other academics.

Biomedical engineering is an exciting field that will change the future of medical technology. If you want to be part of improving our future and saving lives through advancements in medicine, consider a career in mechanical or biomedical engineering.

P.J. VARRASSI, SECURITY ANALYST

There are several booming careers in the computer security industry that you could consider. Explore computer forensics. That's where the future is. These are people who go out into the field to investigate. They pick up a paper trail of how a hacker got into a system and whether they had help.

Newer software such as "Encase" has helped make forensic experts' jobs more exciting. You can take a suspect's computer and download everything that's on there onto a processing machine and forensics unit, which tells you what is on the computer. (If you tried to do it by hand, it would be a nightmare and you undoubtedly would miss much of what's there.)

If you're interested in pursuing a computer security career you should consider obtaining math or computer degrees. It is difficult to become an analyst right out of college. Many analysts begin as computer programmers.

Contact one or more of several professional organizations. I have been a member of most of these organizations. They are an integral part of security. Some groups to consider include High Technology Crime Investigation Association, of which I was an officer for two years, at www.htcia.org, and InfraGard at www.infragard.net.

RECOMMENDED READING

Ada, The Enchantress of Numbers: A Selection from the Letters of Lord Byron's Daughter and Her Description of the First Computer, narrated and edited by Betty A. Toole. Strawberry Press, 1992. (Traces the intellectual development of Ada Lovelace, who is credited with inventing the first computer program, through her letters.)

Computer Crime: Phreaks, Spies and Salami Slicers, by Karen Judson. Enslow Publishers, Inc., 1994. (A good discussion of some computer crimes, what hackers have done, and why computer security is important.)

Condi: The Condoleezza Rice Story, by Antonia Felix. Newmarket Press, 2002. (A biography of the first woman to be named National Security Adviser.)

Cuckoo's Egg: Tracking A Spy Through The Maize of Computer Espionage, by Clifford Stoll. Pocket Books, 2000. (The story of how one man tracked down a computer spy who was out to do a lot of damage.)

Cyber Crimes, by Gina De Angelis. Chelsea House Publishers, 2000. (Explains the various types of cyber crimes, including robbery, terrorism, and pornography, and explores some institutions with "cybercops.")

Cybersafety: Surfing Safely Online, by Joan Vos MacDonald. Enslow Publishers, Inc., 2001. (A good primer on how to stay safe and secure on the Internet.)

Girls & Young Women Inventing: Twenty True Stories About Inventors Plus How You Can Be One Yourself, by Frances A. Karnes and Suzanne M. Bean. Free Spirit Publishing, 1995. (Stories of girls who have invented all types of things, including a computer program for voice recognition.)

The Technology Book for Girls and Other Advanced Beings, by Trudee Romanek. Kids Can Press, 2001. (Explores the use of technology in every-day objects such as CD players, self-flushing toilets, and microwave ovens.)

WEBSITES TO EXPLORE

There are many Internet sites that deal with information security and physical security. Here are some places to start exploring. Many security organizations have addresses outside the United States and some organizations are not appropriate for young readers just beginning to explore such careers. The organizations listed offer programs you may be interested in.

HTTP://WWW.ISTS.DARTMOUTH.EDU

The Institute for Security Technology Studies and its core program on cybersecurity and information infrastructure protection research serve as a principal national center for counterterrorism technology research, development, and assessment.

HTTP://WWW.CERIAS.PURDUE.EDU

The Center for Education and Research in Information Assurance and Security, or CERIAS, at Purdue University, is one of the world's foremost university centers for multidisciplinary research and education in information security. Areas of research include computer, network, and communications security as well as information assurance.
http://www.cerias.purdue.edu/education/k-12/ is a good starting place to learn about security. Interested kids can ask their teachers to have a representative from CERIAS visit their class and give a security workshop designed for elementary, middle school, or high school students.

HTTP://WWW.COMPUTERCAMPS.COM

Information about computer camps. This is a good place to learn about computers in general and to meet adult mentors.

HTTP://WWW.CYBERGRRL.COM

Useful resource site for girls interested in computers. Select "Tech Sections."

HTTP://MATH.RICE.EDU/~LANIUS/CLUB/

Contains a number of links about sites for girls interested in computer science.

HTTP://WWW.AUTODESK.COM/DYF/DYFMAIN2.HTML

Site for girls interested in math, science, and technology with a number of useful resource links.

HTTP://WWW.GENDER.CISCOLEARNING.ORG

Cisco Systems-sponsored program to increase participation of girls and women in computer technology.

HTTP://CS-WWW.NCSL.NIST.GOV

The Computer Security Division is one of eight divisions within the National Institute for Standards and Technology's Information Technology (IT) Laboratory. The Division's mission is to improve information systems security by raising awareness of IT risks, vulnerabilities, and protection requirements, particularly for new and emerging technologies; researching, studying, and advising agencies of IT vulnerabilities and devising techniques for the cost-effective security and privacy of sensitive federal systems; developing standards, metrics, tests, and validation programs; and developing guidance to increase secure IT planning, implementation, management, and operation.

HTTP://WEBOPEDIA.INTERNET.COM

This online encyclopedia dedicated to computer technology is useful if you want to look up the meaning of a computer term. See especially http://webopedia.internet.com/TERM/I/IPsec.html, which has information about security technologies.

HTTP://WWW.INFOSECNEWS.COM

This online newsletter by the publishers of *SC Magazine* provides the latest news about developments in computer security.

HTTP://WWW.SARC.COM/AVCENTER/HOAX.HTML

This website, hosted by Symantec, has information about the latest e-mails that warn of viruses that don't really exist.

HTTP://WWW.BBN.COM/COLLEGE/

BBN Technologies, a high-tech company that has many computer security products and services, has a program to help college students finance their computer education and intern with the company.

HTTP://WWW.FTC.GOV/BCP/CONLINE/EDCAMS/INFOSECURITY/INDEX.HTML

The Federal Trade Commission has created this website for consumers and businesses as a source of information about computer security and safeguarding personal information.

HTTP://WWW.NSA.GOV/ISSO/PROGRAMS/NIETP/NEWSPG1.HTM

The National Security Administration recognizes university centers of excellence for security education and training.

HTTP://WWW.NWCET.ORG/

The National Workforce Center for Emerging Technologies has information about careers in security and other computer fields.

HTTP://WWW.ITAA.ORG/INFOSEC

The Information Technology Association of America has a section on its website for computer security professionals.

PROFESSIONAL ORGANIZATIONS

There are numerous professional organizations that address aspects of security. Some of them are listed below. Search the Internet under "security organizations" to find others.

AMERICAN SOCIETY FOR INDUSTRIAL SECURITY (ASIS)

1625 Prince Street
Alexandria, VA 22314-2818
http://www.asis.org

COMPUTER EMERGENCY RESPONSE TEAM (CERT)

Software Engineering Institute
Carnegie Mellon University
Pittsburgh, PA 15213-3890
http://www.cert.org

COMPUTER SECURITY INSTITUTE (CSI)

600 Harrison Street
San Francisco, CA 94107
http://www.gocsi.com

COMPUTING RESEARCH ASSOCIATION

1100 17th Street NW, Suite 507
Washington, DC 20036-4632
http://www.cra.org

ELECTRONIC PRIVACY INFORMATION CENTER

1718 Connecticut Ave. N.W., Suite 200
Washington, DC 20009
(202) 483-1140

The Forum of Incident Response and Security Teams (FIRST)

PMB 349
650 Castro Street, Suite 120
Mountain View, CA 94041
http://www.first.org

High-Tech Computer Investigations Association (HTCIA)

1474 Freeman Drive
Amisville, VA 20106
http://www.htcia.org

Information Systems Security Association (ISSA)

7044 S. 13th Street
Oak Creek, WI 53154
http://www.issa.org

Information Systems Security Certification Consortium

860 Worcester Road, Suite 101
Framingham, MA 01702
http://www.isc2.org

How COOL Are You?!

Cool girls like to DO things, not just sit around like couch potatoes. There are many things you can get involved in now to benefit your future. Some cool girls even know what careers they want (or think they want).

Not sure what you want to do? That's fine, too... the Cool Careers series can help you explore lots of careers with a number of great, easy to use tools! Learn where to go and to whom you should talk about different careers, as well as books to read and videos to see. Then, you're on the road to cool girl success!

Written especially for girls, this series tells what it's like today for women in all types of jobs with special emphasis on nontraditional careers for women. The upbeat and informative pages provide answers to questions you want answered, such as:

✔ **What jobs do women find meaningful?**
✔ **What do women succeed at today?**
✔ **How did they prepare for these jobs?**
✔ **How did they find their job?**
✔ **What are their lives like?**
✔ **How do I find out more about this type of work?**

Each book profiles ten or eleven women who love their work. These women had dreams, but didn't always know what they wanted to be when they grew up. Zoologist Claudia Luke knew she wanted to work outdoors and that she was interested in animals, but she didn't even know what a zoologist was, much less what they did and how you got to be one. Elizabeth Gruben was going to be a lawyer until she discovered the world of Silicon Valley computers and started her own multimedia company. Mary Beth Quinn grew up in Stowe, Vermont, where she skied competitively and taught skiing. Now she runs a ski school at a Virginia ski resort. These three women's stories appear with others in a series of career books for young readers.

The Cool Careers for Girls series encourages career exploration and broadens girls' career horizons. It shows girls what it takes to succeed, by providing easy-to-read information about careers that young girls may not have considered because they didn't know about them. They learn from women who are in today's workplace—women who know what it takes today to get the job.

ORDER FORM

TITLE	PAPER	CLOTH	QUANTITY
Cool Careers for Girls in Computers	$12.95	$19.95	
Cool Careers for Girls in Sports	$12.95	$19.95	
Cool Careers for Girls with Animals	$12.95	$19.95	
Cool Careers for Girls in Health	$12.95	$19.95	
Cool Careers for Girls in Engineering	$12.95	$19.95	
Cool Careers for Girls in Food	$12.95	$19.95	
Cool Careers for Girls in Construction	$12.95	$19.95	
Cool Careers for Girls in Performing Arts	$12.95	$19.95	
Cool Careers for Girls in Air and Space	$12.95	$19.95	
Cool Careers for Girls in Law	$12.95	$19.95	
Cool Careers for Girls as Environmentalists	$12.95	$19.95	
Cool Careers for Girls as Crime Solvers	$12.95	$19.95	
Cool Careers for Girls in Travel & Hospitality	$13.95	$21.95	
Cool Careers for Girls in Cybersecurity & Nat'l Safety	$13.95	$21.95	
		SUBTOTAL	

VA Residents add 4½% sales tax

Shipping/handling $5.00+ $5.00

$1.50 for each additional book order (__ x $1.50)

TOTAL ENCLOSED _____

SHIP TO: (street address only for UPS or RPS delivery)

Name: _____

Address: _____

❏ I enclose check/money order for $ _____ made payable to Impact Publications

❏ Charge $ _____ to: ❏ Visa ❏ MasterCard ❏ AmEx ❏ Discover

Card #: _____ Expiration: _____

Signature: _____ Phone number: _____

Phone toll-free at 1-800/361-1055, or fax/mail/email your order to:

IMPACT PUBLICATIONS 9104 Manassas Drive, Suite N, Manassas Park, VA 20111-5211

Fax: 703/335-9486; email: info@impactpublications.com